SWEAT

A Practical Plan For Keeping Your Heart Intact While Loving An Addict

by

Denise Krochta

First published by Dog Ear Publishing
4010 W. 86th Street, Ste H
Indianapolis, IN 46268
www.dogearpublishing.net

ISBN: 978-160844-346-8

This book is printed on acid-free paper.

Printed in the United States of America

Introduction

If you have picked up this book, you are looking for something. You are either new to this subject or frustrated about it being a long, ongoing part of your life. Wherever you are in this journey, you are not alone, and you will see, there are choices.

The moment I learned of my son's drug addiction, I immediately, yet quietly, began my search for answers. I felt embarrassed and fearful, and needed to get information without letting this "secret" get out. I was stressed enough. Now I had added stress searching for answers without feeling comfortable asking questions. My hope for all who read this book is that this and many other stress factors can be less. So, the absolute first thing I searched for was knowledge about drug addiction and how to fix it. Before you go any further into this book, I suggest you turn to the reference pages Chapter 13 and look at the Web sites I list. The intention of this book is to cut through the volumes and months of time and materials I already researched and to present to you, the reader, a kind of "cut to the chase" approach to arm you with tools to help you to have a good life no matter the choices of your loved ones. I know from my experience that the first thing you need is knowledge of addiction and what to expect. There will only be a few Web sites on my list, but they are full of the best and current information related to addiction and recovery. This book is not about curing our addicts, but at the moment of "impact," I know that is what we think our priorities are. We quickly become addicted to our addicts and lose focus on anything else. I hope my carefully chosen reference materials, which I will talk briefly about in the body of this book, will save you time, lessen fear and anxiety, and give you a plan for better choices.

Sweat is not a book about drug addiction and about drug addicts. For those who love addicts and alcoholics, you know that one of their characteristics is "it's all about me." *Sweat* is all about us, those of us who love and have loved and lost addicts and alcoholics. It is of hope and serenity and "having a life." It is a book of choice.

Although I experienced enough loss in my life at an early age, nothing prepared me for my son's drug addiction. The first part of *Sweat* is a brief presentation of the setting and "qualifier" for the rest of the book. I'm sure you will all be able to relate to this section. I do not intend for this to be another story about an addict's journey or of the journey of the family addicted to the addict. Our libraries and bookstores are full of those. This is a book of hope. This is a plan of action.

The second part of the book is the "meat" of the book. I have tried to keep everything short and simple. This is my recipe for sanity. My hope is, after reading this book, there will be less hopelessness in your lives and a sense of calm. There are resources in the book that

I have limited to those I found the most useful, related to help available for your addict and understanding the disease itself. Knowledge in this area can be scary, but it is necessary to understand. This is a book of experience, not advice. When I learned of my son's addiction, I had lots of questions, and whatever answers were available were scattered everywhere. The whole process of learning became stressful. My hope is that *Sweat* can alleviate at least that part of the stress in your life and get you centered and calm before the calamity tries to set in.

The third part of the book is kind of a testimonial to how this all has worked for me. I have taken a few crisis events and written about them in relationship to my new perspective and transformation.

My sons are as important to me as are anyone's children to them. I believe I am closer to them than ever. After working very hard at this transformation and making the choices I have made over the past few years, I know that it has made a marked impact on my family and our relationships to each other. My recovery from addiction to my addict began much earlier than my son's recovery from addiction to drugs. My hope for everyone is that no matter what chaos is in your lives at the moment, you are able to control what goes on within you and have some peace. I read somewhere that there will always be sadness, but misery is a choice. I have come to believe this. We can't wait for others around us to make good choices (sometimes they never will), but we can always control our choices. Let *Sweat* guide you to some good choices during difficult times, whether they be with illness, chronic diseases, or addiction. Hopefully, this will help you to create your own habits and exercises to lead you to live fully, despite how others around you have chosen to live.

We all have but one life, our own.

PART ONE

THE QUALIFIER

"When it gets dark enough,
you can see the stars."
—Charles A. Beard

CHAPTER ONE

The bedroom is dark, although it is the middle of a bright, sunny Florida day. I think this bedroom is always dark. There is a navy blue fleece blanket covering the only window in the room. The air is stale with an unfamiliar odor. The king-sized water bed is piled with pillows and blankets and other random objects that don't really belong. There are protein bars and granola bars next to tinfoil, pens, and matches. The bed is familiar but strange. It used to be mine. There are books and papers thrown everywhere. Drawers and cabinets are open as if the place had just been ransacked. Maybe it was. This is how my son had left it after he heard his college roommate was arrested for drug possession on his way back to school from winter break. Obviously, his own exit was quick. He feared he could be next. Did I know my son was a drug addict? Really, the thought never crossed my mind.

The bed takes up half of the room. It is pushed up into the corner against the two adjoining walls. The computer desk and cabinet are on the wall across from the foot of the bed. There is barely room for the desk chair between the desk and the bed. There is a tiny bedside table with a small, dim lamp on it. A recliner rounds out the room. Everything is very close together. There is a walk-in closet and a small bathroom adjacent to the room. The bathroom in the room turns out to be quite convenient. The bedroom is upstairs in the apartment. Just outside the bedroom door is a long hall. In the hall is a small refrigerator with water and juice in it. This, also, turns out to be convenient.

My son has chosen to detox and go through withdrawal from prescription pills (and whatever other substances I don't know) without medical help and a program. Because I love him, I decide to support him in his decision. I think this is the right thing to do. He does not want to participate in a medically supervised inpatient program. That would not allow him to continue and finish his semester at school. In retrospect, this thinking is ludicrous.

So, there we are, both scared, ignorant, and unaware of what we are about to experience. He climbs into bed. After having the "runs" for about two hours, he is ready for some rest. He has a difficult time getting comfortable. He sits up. He rolls over and pulls his knees up, I guess to ease his abdominal pain. Now I know why he has lost so much weight and is sick so often. His body is shaking. I don't know if it is from his crying or from chills. I decide to climb into bed with him and hold him. I am instantly holding my infant son, who was distressed at birth, a very quick but difficult birth. The anesthesiologist was on call that night but not in the hospital. There was no time for him to get there, and there was no time for medication. The baby needed "out" to breathe. The doctor sliced me and grabbed him. It seemed like they were stitching me forever. The boy was fine. Just trouble for Mom. The boys are always fine. Back in the room, the nurses were offering morphine. They said it was normal medication for this kind of trauma. I opted for Tylenol. I wanted to nurse my new baby. It was important to me. No morphine. The baby shouldn't miss any nursing, and I wouldn't think of passing drugs onto my son. Another ludicrous thought.

I try to comfort my grown son. I take a corner of the sheet and wipe the tears from his eyes and the sweat from his brow. One minute he's shaking from chills, the next minute he's hot and feverish. He begins to sob.

Now, I'm holding my one-year-old son, who was determined to learn to walk that day and fell and smacked the back of his head on the beautiful black, blue, and gray terrazzo floors at our old Florida house on the river. I hold him closer and hear his heart racing. I realize his crying is not about his sore head but about cramps and pain in his stomach.

He jumps out of the bed into the bathroom, and I'm jolted back to the present. The bed is wet with his sweat. It is wet with his tears and mine. I hear him vomiting in the bathroom and wonder if this is the beginning or the end. I'm distracted by a banging on the front door downstairs. I wonder, is it the police looking for him? Is it someone wanting to buy drugs? Is it someone coming to collect money? I can't believe these thoughts are even entering my mind. I know the door is locked, and I ignore the banging. Eventually, whoever it is goes away.

My son comes out of the bathroom, face washed, hair slicked back, with a sheepish smile on his face. "Sorry, Mom," he says, and climbs back into bed. How much is this "sorry" supposed to cover? Sorry I started using drugs? Sorry I stole money and things from you and the family? Sorry I destroyed the peace and serenity of our family? Sorry I wasted all the money you spent on college? Sorry I've destroyed my health? Sorry! Sorry! Sorry! Soon he is snoring, and I try to get some sleep. This, of course, is not going to happen. Little do I know that this is to be the beginning of two long years without sleep. Just as I'm beginning to drift off, I hear a scream. It is a terrifying scream followed by deep sobs that shake the water bed as if we were out on the high seas on a stormy night. I grab him. He grabs me. We are trying to save each other from drowning. Nothing I say or do can stop his sobbing. He holds me tighter, and I pull him closer. I am reminded of when both my boys were babies, and I hugged them so tight because I loved them so much, I thought their heads might pop right off! He cries and speaks words that are unintelligible. It scares me. I'm afraid he is losing his mind. I'm afraid I am losing mine, too. He is up, again, into the bathroom. This time I can hear the shower going. It is quiet for what seems an unusually long time. What is he doing in there? Is he still alive? Are there drugs in there? Is this all for nothing? I really don't know the answer to these questions. I wait. He comes out of the bathroom, once again, with his face washed and hair slicked back. He gets back into bed and wants to talk. He speaks about his addiction. He tells me what he thinks these drugs are doing for him, how he got started, how it escalated, and how hooked he really is. He cries in my arms and falls asleep. The darkness is constant. The stagnant air is making me claustrophobic. I want to get out for some air. I imagine a balmy breeze kissing my face with the sound of the palm trees swishing in the wind. But, I'm afraid to leave. I'm not sure why.

It's difficult to say what day it is or what time it is. The hours, days, pass. I survive on water and granola bars, which happen to be living under the pillows. My son can't eat anything. I make him drink water. We talk about life and death. He describes his pain, both physical and mental. Some of his stories are severely distorted perceptions of reality. But, he truly believes them. He sleeps. He vomits. I rub a cool, wet cloth across his brow during his fever and cover him and hold him close during his chills.

During some quiet time when he is resting, I remember something relatively ironic. The day was special. All of the elementary school kids were gathered into the "cafetorium" to honor the winner of the D.A.R.E. essay contest. D.A.R.E., the national Drug Abuse Resistance Education program, sponsored this contest for the fifth-graders each year. Representatives from the sheriff's department and the special D.A.R.E. officers were on hand to present the prize. They had selected three essays from those submitted by the fifth-grade class, a little over a hundred kids, and were to choose the best one at the event. The three kids were up on stage looking very "cleaned up" and proud. There were two girls and one boy. The boy was my son. Each of the three semifinalists read their essays to the audience. I distinctly remember one of the girl's essays being extremely complicated and long. Everyone thought for sure hers would be the winning essay. She was the one who won every writing competition. My son read his essay, which was short and sweet. I don't think it covered more than a page and a half. He smiled his signature smile and fidgeted up on the stage waiting for the result. When the sheriff announced that the "young man" was the winner, everyone clapped and my son was so proud! Of course, I was as well! He put the first-place medal around his neck and beamed with pleasure. The prizes were really to be envied. He won a black jacket with a big red D.A.R.E. on it. There was a hat with the logo on it. Numerous gift certificates from local businesses came in a nice little bag. They saved the best for last. One of the local sheriff's deputies approached the stage with a picture of the prize. It was a picture of a helicopter. He was a helicopter pilot for the sheriff's department. The lucky winner was awarded a ride in his helicopter.

A few days later, my son and my husband flew over the neighborhood surrounding the school in the helicopter. All of the kids in the fifth grade, maybe all of the kids in the school, I don't remember, went out into the adjacent field. They formed letters, like a marching band would do during a football game, to spell his name. He could see it from the helicopter. We still have the framed collage hanging in our den from that day. It is a 25" x 20" wood frame that includes a large color picture of the officer buckling my son into the helicopter. His first-place D.A.R.E. medal is hanging from the picture. There is a small picture that he took of his classmates on the field below in the formation of his name. Another large color picture was taken as he was landing onto the field and is included, with two D.A.R.E. "trading cards." This was to be a day he would never forget! As you can see, I have not forgotten it, either.

Although I'd like to stay tuned to these pleasant memories, I bring myself back to the matter at hand. My son is no longer the little boy whose priority was never to do anything that would put him in "time-out." Now, I think he's leaning more to not getting caught and going to jail. I turn my attention back to my son and his restless sleep.

Most of the time, I don't know what he is thinking or where he really is. When I think things are getting better, there is more vomiting, diarrhea, chills, sweats, delirium, hallucinations, then calm and rest. These all cycle for about three days, I think. On the fourth day, it is time to make a plan. My son is feeling better, although he looks like he has just been pulled off a sinking ship. Who knows what I look like? Really, who cares?

CHAPTER TWO

Six months before this all went down I had put a deposit on a small apartment in Paris. The plan was to escape for a month to one of my favorite places on earth. At the time I placed the deposit I didn't realize the scope the escape would be. My younger son would be up at school, and my older son was spending a year studying in Paris. My husband was busy at the office, so I thought this would be a good plan. When I was younger, I had a career in international business and had been to Paris numerous times. Although I have a degree in French and learned a lot about the country during all my years of study, there were many things I wanted to learn about first hand. During my times of work there, I really didn't get a chance to see much.

When my kids were in their teens, we would go as a family on vacation and often spend a few days in Paris. It was fun with the family, but it was a different discovery process than what I had in mind. I was very excited about doing it in my own time. I hoped to really soak up the ambiance and learn of interesting Paris secrets on my own. I thought it might be a good thing to do while my son was studying there. I had hopes that I would see him more than once that year since I would be living in the same city for a month. I really looked forward to April in Paris!

After my harrowing and sad experience with my younger son up at school, I began to have second thoughts about this long-planned trip. Did I really want to be that far away from this tenuous situation? My son was up at school telling me that he was not using drugs, he was attending self-help meetings, and visiting a school psychologist. Did I really trust all that? No, not really. I felt obligated to cancel my trip and stay home. Stay at home and do what, exactly? Worrying and being fearful about what he was doing four hours away at college could be done from an apartment in Paris. I could obsess about how I might have caused all this and how I was going to fix it, also from an apartment in Paris. I could even relive, over and over, those days in his room at school in an apartment in Paris. So, I couldn't decide. I knew what I wanted to do, but what would be the right thing? I soon learned, when it comes to dealing with addicted loved ones, there really is no right or wrong, really no answers.

A few weeks before I would be going to Paris, another sad thing happened in our family. The family dog, a nine-year-old boxer, had to be put to sleep because of a neurological problem. My younger son, who was very close to her, came down from school, and we all took her in and said good-bye. It was a sad day for all of us. Was my son using drugs to kill his pain and sadness? I don't know. I was in denial and cautiously optimistic at the time. I was sad about the dog—she was my constant companion—and couldn't really tell the difference between grief and drugs at the time. My son went back to school, and the house was very quiet without the boys and the dog. Against my guilty conscience and, frankly, against my perceived judgment of those around me, I continued on with my plan and landed in Paris on April Fool's Day. I tried to dismiss the irony of this and put on a happy face for my older son, who seemed genuinely glad to see me. We had last seen each other during the winter holidays, just before our family chaos began. Guilt and fear were my traveling companions, but breathing in that Paris air kept them in my pocket, momentarily.

By late afternoon I was settled in my new Paris home. It was time to breathe and take it all in. The apartment was very small but perfect for me. It was in a very old building on the Left Bank. To enter I had to walk up three stories of a tiny spiral staircase. It was quite quirky, actually. The ceilings were tall, and there were tall windows in the living/dining/kitchen area. Outside the windows were tiny balconies with pots of geraniums. The front of the building was on a pedestrian street. It was a cobblestone street with gas lights for street lamps. There were restaurants down below next door and across the street. The street smelled wonderful! The bedroom was small but comfortable, and the tall window opened up overlooking an inner courtyard.

My son had gone home to do some work and let me get settled and relax a bit after my long journey. I decided to go out and check out the neighborhood and buy a few groceries. I could tell the neighborhood was just what I was looking forward to, and I remembered it from some of the trips with the family. So, it was familiar. When I got back to the apartment I put the groceries away and put the flowers in water and sat down. It had been a long two days. It was at that moment that I remembered. All my insecurities about my addicted son began to inundate my mind. Here I was in a strange place, very far away from holding my boy, not knowing if he was alive or dead, and I couldn't do anything about it. I asked myself why I did this crazy thing coming so far away, and I just started to sob. I couldn't stop crying. I was frustrated, sad, scared, fearful, and even a bit angry that my son had ruined my trip. Was this selfish? At the time, I did beat myself up quite a bit about it until I settled myself down. I later discovered that this is what loving an addict does. We begin to question our judgment. We spend our time addicted to the addict. I did this when I found out about his problem until the time I got on the plane to Paris. I had hoped that my excitement and wonder could overshadow these insecurities. There certainly wasn't any reason for me not to do this. It was going to be a long 30 days if I didn't snap myself out of it. I also owed it to my older son to be happy to see him and learn about his life in Paris. I tried to make some order out of all of this. I knew I could be in Paris but not experience Paris if I didn't figure out a way out of my funk. So, I made a deal with myself that I tried to keep, and although I deviated from it here and there, I was able to save my vacation and accomplish much of what I had planned.

The deal was this. I would dedicate a small amount of time in the morning to thinking about my son and his situation. I would be fearful and sad and then I would try to leave it behind me for the day. Paris was exciting and I could do this most days. I heard from home almost every day. When there was news of my son, it usually wasn't good. I remember one time he had gone home for the weekend and my husband had surprised him with a drug test from the local drugstore. He tested positive, but explained it all with something about a cold and cough medicine. Did any of us believe this? I don't think it really mattered. Sometimes I even got an overseas call from my son at college. What could I really tell over the phone? More of that later.

This is not a travel guide. Suffice it to say, April in Paris is a wonderful experience. I am including this chapter to emphasize the impact addiction can have no matter what is going on in each of our lives. So, I tried my best to focus on and enjoy my time in Paris. The dinners I shared with my older son were really enjoyable. I felt close to him and wished one day to have that feeling again with his brother. I really didn't know for sure that relapse had occurred, but I had my suspicions. My days were all interesting and each different than the one before. The only constant was the time I spent worrying about addiction. It was all still relatively new to me, and I was still wondering about my role in all of this and what I, as a mom, was able to do about it. If I could just love him out of it, that would be a piece of cake. So, I thought about it in the morning and before I went to bed at night. It snuck up on me in the strangest places during the day, but I got to be pretty good at dismissing it then.

I do remember a time I did not succeed. This was a very strange experience for me. I was planning on spending the day at a local museum, not far from my home. It was a rainy Sunday, a perfect museum day. The museum used to be called the Cluny, but the name had been changed to the Museum of the Middle Ages. I had been through it in the past but never got to really see it. This was my chance. The rooms were numbered. There were many of them. There was a brochure describing what was in each room, but it looked like it would be interesting to just go through in order, not skipping to certain exhibits. I had the entire day and I was alone, with no one to prod me on.

I was brought up Catholic, and my family was very involved in the church. My mom worked for the priest, and both my parents did lots of volunteering while we were growing up. Sundays were days spent first at mass; then the entire family—cousins, aunts and uncles, brothers, sisters, sometimes priests and nuns—went over to one of the nearby homes of an aunt or uncle for breakfast, and sometimes we spent the entire day there. My mom taught catechism, and it was a big part of our lives. We heard the stories of Christmas, Easter, this saint and that saint, and were quite well-versed in most things Catholic. There was something in my perception as a kid that grew with me and bothered me at times. I had this thing about Mary, the mother of Jesus. I really am not going to delve into religious beliefs here, but I think this story has some bearing on this whole process. My perception had always been that although this woman was always portrayed as a saint and forgiving, blessed, and all kinds of good things, it always seemed to me that there wasn't really much about her and the relationship she had with her son when he became a man. I always wondered why we didn't really see her around much in his "heyday," so to speak. This always bothered me but just in the back of my mind.

This museum had a lot of religious art in it. I spent a lot of time trying to focus on the art and understand where the artist was coming from when I came upon a picture of Mary, and Jesus as an adult. I don't even remember now what the exact picture was about, but I can tell you exactly how I felt during the time I was looking at that picture. I think I was in room 21, so I had already spent a big part of the day in this dark museum. It was a rainy, dreary day, so that also could have added to my mood. But I searched those eyes and the expression on her face, and finally, after 50 years hearing about this woman, I could see her pain and her connection to her son. Was it because I was feeling a similar pain about my son? Was the artist really that good? I don't really know. I do know that, again, I cried and had to leave the museum, with others wondering what went on in room 21. I was, again, touched by my son's addiction.

A few days after this museum episode, my younger son was flying over to spend some time with me after school was out. I would be there for only two days while he was there and then he would spend a week with his brother. I was anxious to see him. I was also a bit scared. He was arriving with his girlfriend, and it all sounded like a very nice plan. The day they arrived I thought he looked good. I hadn't seen him in over a month, and I had high hopes. I wanted him to be in recovery, and I wanted to trust him. I guess I saw what I wanted. Late in the afternoon he fell asleep until the next day. This was not unusual after an overnight flight overseas, and I didn't think anything of it. We had dinner with his brother the night before I was to fly back to the States, and I enjoyed my rare time with my two sons together. A few days after I had returned home, the calls began. My older son was calling to let me know about his younger brother's strange activities there in Paris. He was leaving for hours, without his girlfriend, and returning without answering questions. He began to speak about having back pain and going to doctors. He was never one to enjoy speaking foreign languages, so going to French doctors was really making an effort. My older son became concerned. His brother became distant. It didn't seem like a fun trip anymore. It sounded like he was doctor shopping, and I was wondering exactly what he was shopping for. Now he was the one far away and I was home. It was all very bizarre. Before he came home he called me from Paris. What did I say earlier about not being able to discern anything over the phone? Well, I knew right away from his conversation that chaos was about to return to my world.

CHAPTER THREE

After my son's return from Paris, I had a surprise for him. He had stopped at school and picked up his things to spend the summer at home. He would start his job as soon as he got home. This is what he thought, anyway. I was scared straight, so to speak, and I had other plans for him. When he arrived he emptied his car into his room and disappeared for a while. When he resurfaced I sat him down and told him the plan. I gave him two files to read. One described a rehab facility in our state, and one described one out of state. The phone numbers and program information was all in the files. I told him that he was to choose which one he would be attending, and he would be going as soon as a bed became available. With little resistance, he made calls to both facilities and returned with his choice. I immediately called the facility, the one an hour from where we lived, paid the deposit over the phone, and made arrangements to drive him down the next day.

When I described to the people at the rehab the amount of boxes of pills, empty, that he had brought home with him, they told me how lucky he was to be alive. Yes, chaos had returned. He was to remain there for

30 days, which included his 20th birthday. I drove him down the next day and began 30 days of peace of mind with great expectations. We did our part and visited him each Sunday afternoon. We attended the three-day family weekend that was included in the tuition. Once a week his therapist would call and go over his progress. It was a relaxing month for us except for the visits and calls, which always brought some fear and insecurity back into the moment.

My older son had returned from Paris and was also home for the summer. I think he was a bit taken aback by the change in the energy in the house. This was the first taste he had of living at our home with addiction looming over us. He was not pleased with the change. This did not make for good sibling bonding.

We all missed the dog. When we thought about getting another, my younger son said that after his time at home and when he was well into his recovery he would take the dog to school with him. So, in my enabling way, and being optimistic, I agreed to get another dog, and it would be his dog. When he came home after fulfilling his rehab expectations, there was a new boxer puppy to greet him. She was a bright spot in an otherwise gloomy environment. We tried to be trusting of my son's recovery. Our trust was reserved, I admit. We insisted that both boys work together for the summer and that my older son drive them on work days. He was right when he said he felt like a babysitter. We were wrong to put him in that position. This was more enabling, but we really didn't know any better at the time. So the summer went by quietly enough, and we didn't notice any disasters. We were very nervous, and our trust was limited, but that's what addiction does. We tried to revive our close, happy family, as much as the situation and times would allow, but it just never really felt quite right.

CHAPTER FOUR

"Divine influence is evident when a cluster of disasters occurs in a remarkably short period of time and reroutes your life. The hallmark of a divine experience is that it gets your attention and leads you to think something out of the ordinary is happening to you. Divine encounters will be ongoing, as opposed to a onetime phenomenon."

I was reading through an old book off my shelf in the den when the above fell out. It was in my writing, so I know that at some time in my life I wrote this down because it got my attention. For me life has been a series of tragedies and disasters mixed in with the good times, I guess not unlike the lives of most mortals. This, though, was a fortuitous time for this to fall into my lap.

Uneventful and status quo had become quite a blessing. In the past, illness, crisis, and death were the status quo. When I was a young woman just beginning college, I learned that my six-year-old sister was ill with childhood leukemia. This was back in the 1970s when treatment and cures were limited. Although it was a 14-hour drive from my home those days, I spent as much time back there with my parents and sister as possible. I was drawn to this little girl. She was more than just my little sister at this point. Even though she was so young, she taught me a lot about life, illness, and death. I crammed my degree into three years and raced home as her health failed. I was able to spend a month or so with her before she died. What a way to learn how short life can be! Her death shaped much of my future. It especially played a big part in how I raised my children. Every moment was "golden."

Years later, after I had married and my kids were in grade school, another trauma happened to our family. My older brother, who was a wholehearted participant in the 1970s and 1980s world of rock musicians and the lifestyle that accompanied it, was diagnosed with colon cancer at the age of 38. It was another year of sadness and despair. Again, I was drawn to him to learn as much as I could about him, what he was feeling and thinking, and to just be there for him. Another stressful time reminding me, in case I had forgotten, that life was short, and not one moment should be taken for granted. After his death at the age of 40, I, once again, re-prioritized my values.

So, here I was about ten years later, and maybe I was forgetting these lessons. I guess I needed another wake up call. I wanted to scream, "I'm awake already!"

Addiction came in and disrupted the lives of everyone in my family, separately but equally. We all lost focus on everything but the illness, chaos, and crisis. We all handled things differently and began to distance ourselves from each other. Our family was being pulled apart by this addiction something none of us could control, and all cohesiveness as a family was lost. Chaos became a large part of our daily existence. Eventually, there was a calm, and, after some hard work and rallying together, the energy in the house lifted very slowly to an almost acceptable level. During this time I was reminded again how we have little control over what happens with others. At this point I made a promise to myself to devise a plan that would help me to learn how to focus on controlling myself from within. I wanted to begin making conscious choices to control my perceptions of and reactions to things. I knew it would be a slow process but I began.

It was at this time that we decided that the family needed a little healing, bonding time together. The boys were getting ready to go back to college for the fall semester. We all agreed that a short vacation away from the "heaviness" of our past few months would be a good plan. Fortunately (I'll let you be the judge of this), we live in Florida. The easiest way to get away in the summer quickly and cheaply is to jump on a cruise ship and go to the Caribbean or Mexico. So I found the soonest, least expensive, and agreeable cruise, and we set out. We drove across the state to get on the ship, destination Mexico. Our plan was simple: enjoy each other's company while relaxing. This we did. We saved one of the planned excursions off the boat for our last full day. For those who are not familiar with summer in Florida and the Caribbean, it is extremely hot and humid every day—steamy, I guess you would say. We chose an all-day trip to the ancient Mayan ruins of Tulum. Since these were on the coast, we felt there should be a breeze, and it might be beautiful to see. We dressed in as little clothing as possible that would be socially acceptable and set off with our water bottles. The trip would take two and a half hours to get from the cruise ship to the ruins. When we arrived we walked with the guide toward the main area of the ruins. I couldn't breathe! There was no air. I could feel the sweat tickling my skin as it slowly dripped down my back, down my nose, and on the back of my hands. The guide was relating to us how lucky we were. Yesterday the temperature was 114 degrees. Today it is only 103 degrees! My husband—who loves museums, ruins, historical monuments, really anything old but new to him—was just standing there under a small tree, absorbing all of the information and sites. My sons and I were a bit distracted by the heat and the flies. I knew they were thinking what I was thinking. Where are the cliffs by the water? There's got to be some kind of breeze there, and why aren't we there yet? After a few minutes the guide sent us on our self tours, and I'm sure you know where we headed. We were not the only ones! We climbed up onto the cliffs overlooking the water, and it was quite a beautiful site. The waters off the coast of Mexico are so beautiful. You can almost taste the green-blue of them. There was a breeze, and as we sat on the rocks we were content and somewhat relieved from the intense heat. Soon, my husband decided it was time to explore the ruins. Although in the past our family has been extremely adventurous, he couldn't get us to budge this time. He went off on his own when we promised to follow momentarily. Twenty minutes passed. It was time. My younger son and I decided to go find Dad. My older son decided that he had already seen enough ruins, and he was quite satisfied to lie in the sun on the cliffs and relax. It didn't happen.

Not one minute had passed before I slipped on the salt spray from the water on one of the rocks on my way down, fell and broke my wrist in two places, and became unconscious. As I opened my eyes a few moments later, I heard my son yelling, "Mom, Mom!" So much for a relaxing, healing vacation... After my older son heard the screaming and ran off to find his father, we started on our way back on our two and a half hour journey to find a hospital in the local town near the ship. That experience will be another story. About six hours later, just in time to get back to the ship before it left for home, we arrived back on the ship. My right arm was covered from my armpit to the tips of my fingers with a neon pink, hard cast. Enough excitement yet? This was just a kind of sideline to the story. As we climbed the stairs to go to our cabins, we saw a big sign in the main lobby of the ship: "Hurricane Charley on its way to Florida! Possibly a Category 4 hurricane by the time it reaches land!" So, we were following a hurricane back to Florida with a path that was projected to be the same as our route. Lots of opportunity to try my new skills that day!

We had lived in Florida for 20 years and were used to hurricane predictions coming and going. It is usually something we Floridians take in our stride. Another thing we can't control... The weather. But because of the circumstances of that day, I was feeling a bit negative and began to follow the reports with interest. When we arrived into port the next day, the hurricane had, indeed, hit with a vengeance, but its path had veered a bit north and did not do the damage to Tampa, where we had disembarked, that was predicted. It hit a less populated area but was still considered a major hurricane. We had some trouble driving home through debris and downed trees on some of the highways but returned home safely and tried to look at the trip as successful.

The boys began to prepare for their return to college. My older son was to begin his last year and would fly to the New York area in about two weeks time. My younger son would spend a semester at home, attending the local junior college, a slight deviation from his original plan. We thought things were about to get back to some kind of order. Again we were wrong. As the week approached for our older son's departure, the media began its incessant tracking of a storm coming from the tropics. Unless you live in Florida or the Gulf States, you probably don't know how nerve-wracking this is. They begin to announce the coordinates of the storm every hour on the hour. Then there are the pictures of the projected track. You begin to pay attention if your town is within the projected "cone of death," as we so fondly refer to it. Then the preparations begin. No one really wants to go through the trouble of all of the preparations if there will be no hurricane, but this time it looks like the possibility is there. We all scurry to buy batteries for all of the flashlights. We begin to fill water jugs with water every day. We clean what we can out of the freezer to make room for the water jugs in case the power goes out. We stock up on canned goods and think about moving outside furniture into the garage. This is just in case.

As the storm gets near, about three days away, it looks like it is projected to be a very serious Category 3 or 4 hurricane, and the path will take the eye of the storm directly through our town. Now we have to decide what to do. My son's flight leaves from the local airport in two days. Do we want to be in our house in the middle of the eye of the storm? Do we feel lucky? We have a family meeting and decide that we are not going to stay. My parents live on the West Coast (back to Tampa). The storm is projected to just skirt that area, so we could be safe there. The predictions get worse by the hour. We change my son's flight to go out of Tampa. We pack up a few things and decide to head west. By this time almost everyone in south Florida is heading north or west. The highways are like parking lots, and gas stations are running out of gas. There are lines at the turnpike rest areas 100 people long to use the restrooms. The storm is fast approaching, and we turn off to some of the side roads. It takes six and a half hours to go the usual three-hour trip. We feel lucky to arrive safely and before the storm.

During the next 24 hours we watch television to see hurricane Frances pass right through our town as a Category 2 hurricane. We get my son off to the airport just in time for the now-tropical storm to come through the Tampa area. We sit tight and wait. We want to go home to see what is there. The roads are closed, and we are away for five days. When they open some of the roads, we decide to try to get home. The devastation was heart wrenching. It was difficult to believe that the roads we were traveling were the same ones we had traveled regularly over the past 25 years. Most signs and trees were down in the path of the storm. The middle of Florida has miles and miles of cattle ranches. The barns had no roofs, or there were no more barns. Where were all the cattle? Power lines were down everywhere, and as we got closer to our side of the state, things got even worse. There was no power. There were no signs. The streets were full of debris, both from vegetation and buildings. We were in awe of nature. As we approached our community it was difficult to breathe. The air was so still. There were no working streetlights. Our community was rather old and was known for its big yards full of large trees. We had lived there for ten years and never saw most of the homes because they were hidden by trees. Not anymore. Trees, power lines, roofing materials, and trash were strewn everywhere. As we approached our home you could hear everyone in the car catch their breath. The first thing we noticed were our five 40-foot Washingtonian palm trees snapped like pencils, blocking our driveway. We had to park the car at the end and walk up the driveway. It was near evening, and the sun was fading. September in Florida is usually devastatingly hot, and that day was no exception. It was at least 95 degrees. We went into the house. There was not too much damage inside. Most of the damage was outside. Since we were gone for five days, and the power had been out most of that time, there was the smell of things rotting. Our 150 gallon fish tank was full of dead, tropical fish. The food in both of our refrigerators had begun to rot, and there was no air flowing due to no air conditioning. We were grateful for what was still there. We continued out the back door to discover some of the screen porch over the pool had come down, and trees were down everywhere. When we had time to assess the yard damage, we counted 36 landscaped trees were down. There was no power for a few more days. We were lucky; some of our friends got their power back that night and invited us to stay with them. It took three more days until we got power. The cleanup began.

There was no food in the stores for days. They had no power. There was no gas at the gas stations for days. When the trucks finally came to deliver the gas, there was no electricity to pump it. It was a stressful time for us all, especially difficult for me because of the inconvenience of my broken wrist. We had to be very careful when taking the dog outside because she was not used to being careful where she walked. Her stepping on debris and getting cut up was not anything we needed to add to an already difficult situation. It took weeks to get back to some semblance of order. We finally got the trees and debris put into ten-foot piles along the driveway and the road for the trucks to pick up. The power returned, and the smell began to dissipate.

It was at this time, after trying to deal with my son's addiction, my broken wrist, a minor hurricane, and a major hurricane, that I decided to reevaluate my stress level and the general mental health of the family. Things needed to happen, or we were all going to "break." I continued to practice my new work on myself. I canceled my newspapers. The news was too stressful. I knew if there was something important to deal with, someone would tell me. I stopped watching television for the same reason. I dedicated a small amount of time first thing in the morning to connecting to my spirit with some prayer and simple meditation. I tried to get back to my mantra from my early days of trauma to not worry until I had to. I knew I had choices. I chose to be calm.

Just as I was settling into a more positive frame of mind and a regular spirit-lifting ritual, it started all over. It was time to worry again! My son came from school with the news that a new tropical depression had formed, and it was predicted to take the same path as the one that just hit us. Before that was to come Hurricane Ivan, which missed us just that week, had turned back around and was dumping a large amount of rain on us in the form of a tropical storm. What would we do this time? We decided to stay and see what happened. I took a deep breath, thought some positive thoughts, and felt pretty good. I had a sense of calm that surprised me. There was fear but it was not overwhelming. So, it was time to fill the water jugs, bring in the outside furniture, etc. Frances was a slow mover and dumped tons of rain, and now, after Ivan, we really needed to worry about flooding. We now had the extra worry of all the existing debris being loose to blow around. What would it be like to actually be in the middle of a hurricane? We were about to find out. I needed to add to my plan of lessened stress. The hurricane was four days away. One night I filled up the bathtub, which I had never used, and lit some candles, and listened to some uplifting music. I realized that I like this, too. This was relaxing, as long as I didn't think while I was doing it. I took some spiritual and relaxation tapes out of the library and put them on my MP3 player.

I listened to them while walking the dog and even while preparing for the hurricane.

The day came, and it was only a matter of hours. Hurricane Jeanne was on the projected path right to our town. Everything was as prepared as it could be. The cars, bikes, and any loose objects were all locked up tight in the garage. The coolers and freezers were full of ice, and bottles of water were everywhere. Piles of batteries were out on the counters along with every flashlight we could find.

My son, who had suspiciously disappeared for a few hours that day, was back putting the finishing touches on the master bedroom closet with blankets, pillows, more flashlights, batteries, and more water. This was to be our "safe room" for the direct hit; no windows and no outside walls. The power was already out. We began a Monopoly game by lantern. We tried to focus on the game and not the mayhem outside. I had just finished celebrating my purchase of Boardwalk and Park Place when things began to really go sour. It started raining, literally, on Park Place. Was it my imagination or was it raining on me too?

We moved into high gear as we realized that there was water coming into the house in various ways. It was raining from the skylights, and rain was being blown in through the tracks of the sliding glass doors. We grabbed all of the towels and buckets we owned and scrambled all over the house to catch what we could and try to block out the rest. Just as we'd run out of dry towels, we heard on the radio that the worst of the front of the storm was about to hit. We all ran into the closet to be safe. This also was a slow-moving storm. It really did sound like a locomotive coming through the house. It seemed to last forever. The guys fell asleep quickly. I couldn't sleep but did some meditating and relaxation work, then went out to check on the storm.

I could tell that we were now in the eye of the storm. It's hard to predict just how long the eerie silence and calm of the eye will last, so I quickly gathered up the dog and went outside with my flashlight to let her pee. It was difficult to tell what was out there because it was so dark, but there were plenty of neighbors out with their flashlights, trying to assess the damage. We hurried inside, not wanting to get caught in the backside of the storm. Just in time we heard the rain and wind start again. We did not return to the closet. It was just too hot and stuffy for a claustrophobic person like me. So, the pup and I sat on the living room couch and hoped for the best. After about an hour or so, it all seemed calm. We fell asleep, and when the boys woke us up in the morning, we all went out together. Again it was not pretty. This time the damage was more inside. We could see that we'd have to rip up carpeting, fix walls, and clean up mud that somehow entered the house. There was no spoiled food this time, and the fish tank was never fixed and replaced from the last storm, so no dead fish either. We had all survived, and our house was still standing. I had plenty to write in my new gratitude journal. Miracles do happen!

During all of this hustle and bustle, I guess it is not surprising that our recent family crisis had begun again. My son's addiction problem was once again in the forefront of our lives. Our family became unhealthy again, and the storm in my heart matched the storm outside. My new plan was no match for this, but I was determined to be persistent. Life was taking on a new perspective for me. Negative things were happening to me, but I was looking at them in new ways. My perspective had begun to change since I implemented my plan, and I knew that I had help to get through it all. My spirit had become my new best friend. I was learning that nurturing myself was helping me to nurture my family and to deal with any chaos around me. It was all still coming at me in full force, but it was becoming less of a challenge and more of an opportunity. The more I meditated and became still, the better my coping skills became. Over the next few months of chaos and cleanup, both of our physical home and of our breaking family, I was steadfast in keeping to my plan and adding new tools daily. I was able to focus on the moment and be at peace during most of the turmoil. As time passed I became more skilled at using these tools, and even though my life appeared to be tragic, in reality I became more calm and happy. This gave me the opportunity to help my family to get through some of the most difficult times of our lives and live to tell about it.

During the next year of yard and house cleanup, I planted a garden, which I had never done before. I started by up-righting a small hibiscus bush that had been knocked down in one of the storms and had been lying down for months. Each morning I look out into the garden to see what is blooming that day. I can predict the tone of my day by the butterfly activity. It gives me such pleasure. Again, fortunately, we live in Florida with year-round gardens.

In the fall of 2005, we were again hit by a hurricane—Wilma this time. It finished off my pool enclosure and pushed rain inside again. We are still putting things back together. Maybe we always will be. It is all good. I believe that my life was permanently rerouted, and something extraordinary did happen to me from all of this. It is another day in paradise, and I am grateful.

CHAPTER FIVE

So, my older son was back up north at school, out of day-to-day chaos, and we had this new way of life to deal with. Thank goodness for the comic relief of this ornery puppy. Needless to say, she was a lot of work, and it was all up to me. Drug addicts have a difficult time taking care of themselves, so expecting my son to take care of a puppy was unrealistic. Things got worse as my son lived with us and continued his bad choices. We were experiencing all of the anxieties and fears of all people who love addicts. We could see his health deteriorating. I did everything I thought I needed to do. I continuously searched his room, followed him everywhere, grilled him about every moment of his day. Things and money began to go missing, and strange people were coming to our home late at night. Phone calls came in with lots of hang-ups. There was a lot of bad energy in the house. My son was full of anger, conniving and manipulative, and we all handled it differently. I felt like he was holding us ransom in our own home. We had to put locks on our bedroom and closets. We had to buy a safe and keep anything we valued in it. My husband expected me to lock all the bedrooms, bathrooms, and closets each time I took the dog out or went out for the mail. Again, the energy in the house became explosive.

My role in all this began to slowly change. My de-stressing plan had begun to take hold, and my days were less chaotic and more calm. It was good for me, but a puzzle for those around me. In fact, as the days approached the holidays, and we became more involved in the holidays and paid less attention to the addict, things reached a crisis level quickly without us even realizing it. On Christmas Eve the decision was finally made. My son could no longer live with us. Or should I say, we just couldn't take it anymore. There was no waiting for after the holidays. This would be his first Christmas Eve and Christmas without his family. We were sad. I don't think he really cared.

It was a sad holiday for us but, in a way, a relief. We heard of his whereabouts during the holidays, and things were not going well for him. His expectations of being welcomed with open arms were unfounded, and he found himself with big problems. He was desperate to feed his addiction and stole drugs from someone's home. Lucky for him, they gave him the choice to go to a detox facility or to go to jail. He arrived at the detox facility and was to be there for five days. We heard he had left without a doctor's release and was back out on the streets. This is a parent's worst nightmare. There is no sense in getting into the details here. He ended up after the holidays agreeing to go to his earlier rehab to detox and then to go out west to a long-term rehab. He really had no choice. So, again we thought we would have a respite from the chaos. He was to spend five days detoxing and then I would pick him up at the facility and take him right to the airport, and together we would go out to the long-term rehab three thousand miles from home.

On the third day, they called from the rehab and told me I had to go and get him. Although he was not yet fully detoxed he was being asked to leave. He was selling drugs to other treatment patients. There was no bed for him at the new rehab out west for two more days, and I didn't really want him back at the house. But he was my son and I love him. I picked him up with a calm reserve. I used some of my new tools to calm myself. I really needed to be calm through this incident. He was wreaking havoc at the rehab, and the nurses were expecting a frantic mother in denial. That, I guess, is what they are used to. They remarked at least twice how much they appreciated my attitude and calm. They couldn't really believe what they saw, actually. We went home and my husband and I basically kept him under guard until we got on the plane two days later. It was a very unpleasant trip for both of us. For me, I had to deal with his anger and frustration. He had to deal with nausea and diarrhea from not being detoxed and not having drugs. I'm sure the scenario would have been different if he was feeling well. My son is over six feet tall, and I am just over five feet two inches. I was lucky he was too ill to bolt. My son was no longer welcome to live with us, and there was a gradual return of normalcy to our home.

PART TWO

PLANNING PEACE

*"There are only two ways to live your life.
One is as though nothing is a miracle. The
other is as though everything is a miracle."*
Albert Einstein

CHAPTER SIX

The plan to reclaim my life began even before my son acknowledged his need to do the same and enter long-term rehab. We rewind here to mid chaos.

Months went by and the days seemed the same. I pretended to live as a human and part of society. It was all a ruse. My days consisted of sitting, no matter where I happened to be, and thinking about all of my fears and anxieties related to my son's addiction. There was no focus on anything else. The nonprofit I ran had to run on its own as much as possible, and others had to pick up the slack, not knowing why. Who wants to talk about their son's drug addiction and be judged? I felt guilty but had no energy to focus. Bills weren't getting paid, and daily chores weren't getting done. The only family member who got any attention was the addict. How did this make the rest of the family feel? At the time I didn't have the energy to care. The only thing I thought about or cared about was will my son still be alive tomorrow? I focused only on the "what-ifs."

One day it hit me. The headaches I never had before in my life were getting more severe and frequent. I was putting on weight from not working out and eating poorly. I was on edge every time the phone rang or the door opened. This was not me, just who I had become. It occurred to me that, one day, my son and the other addicts in my life might, hopefully, find their way and become happy, productive members of society. At the rate I was going, I might be too sick or dead to enjoy them. I realized this was about the only thing under my control. I decided to pull myself up and learn how (as instructed in an old Paul Simon song) to "dominate the impossible in my life."

Instead of sitting and focusing on my son, I slowly switched over to my new goal. I began to frequent my local library and practically inhale everything I could find on the necessary subjects. I began with stress relief information. Understand that my focus was minimal and my attention span minute. The research I did was unique and quite different from my usual in-depth and specific digging I have been used to in the past. I was in international business for a long time and worked with customs and licensing. It was a very detailed way of looking at things, necessary but tedious. No, this was basic information easily understood by the masses. My brain could only work this way now.

I read books on enabling, addictive minds, self-preservation while surrounded by chaos, simple meditation, books written by addicts for addicts, books by therapists, etc. I went to seminars by addiction specialists. I read about different rehab philosophies and became a regular at a local support group for families and friends of drug addicts. I weeded through volumes of books, magazines, CDs, DVDs, and newspapers, actually becoming addicted to learning to live with this and come out on top.

So, as the days went by, I was able to take some attention away from living my drug addict son's life and begin to live my own. Just learning and planning to do something to get my life back was actually a therapeutic beginning to my plan.

As I mentioned above, I found a local group that had meetings once a week and began to attend. I immediately felt relief by just being somewhere for an hour a week where I could pay attention to others' stories, take my mind off my problems, and be somewhere where I didn't have to explain anything. They all knew. Also, I listened intently and often heard stories that were much worse than mine, and in a sick kind of way, it made me feel better. This particular group happened to be a 12-step program. This is not what attracted me and is not the key to what kept me going. It is absolutely not necessary to be a believer in the 12-step philosophy to get benefit from these groups. The steps are there if you want them. This kind of group was really the only "help" available I found that was not cost prohibitive and required no effort. With my frame of mind, there was no way I was capable of doing anything that took a lot of effort and socializing on my part. So, this was the first step I took, and I think it was a good start. The group will let you know right at the beginning that its purpose is to help others get their lives back and learn to take care of themselves. It is not a place to learn how to cure and control addicts.

Lots of time was spent organizing books and other materials and choosing which ideas to try and which to discard. I read volumes of books on simple meditation. It wasn't until I stopped reading about it and actually tried it that I realized what an impact such a simple thing, practiced a few minutes a day, could do. Meditation, for someone who has no focus, is not an easy thing. I remember trying what seemed to be one of the simplest meditations I found. The plan was to go out and take a walk and count my steps as I walked. When I got to 100 steps counted without losing my focus on counting, I could go home. If I lost my focus, I would need to start counting from the number one. Well, the first time I tried this, I walked for an hour and a half and never got to 100 without losing focus. The beauty of this exercise was that, although I kept letting my mind drift back to my son and his problems, for the moments I was counting, my mind was pretty much empty of stress and fear. More on all this as we get into the Plan.

Because of the problem with focus (on anything other than fear), I began to write a lot of things down. This became a necessity. This also became an escape. I learned about the value of writing things down "for later." I began to journal. I was shocked and amazed, when I reread my previous thoughts, how much I learned about myself. This part of the Plan is one of the most valuable for me. It merits a chapter all its own.

So, my son's addiction continued, I began to devise this plan, and I noticed our relationship changing. I had choices and he had choices. He continued to make bad choices, and I slowly began to make better ones. This is important to emphasize here. Nothing had changed in the whole scheme of the addiction, yet my days seemed very different and better. I was slowly beginning to see how choices and perceptions play a very interesting role in how our days go and just how life is.

Speaking of writing things down. It was at this time I decided to actually organize, into a very simple list, what tools I had read about that seemed worth trying and those I already had tried that worked for me. I wanted to feel healthier (body, mind, and spirit). I wanted to feel some peace and serenity for at least a part of every day. I wanted to practice ways to keep my wits about me when chaos was claiming everyone else. And so I organized and reorganized. I prioritized and reprioritized. When I finally was satisfied with my choices, I chose a few to focus on and see what happened. Over the next few weeks, fortunately or unfortunately, I had the opportunity, repeatedly, to see how things were going and its effect in the middle of chaos. My life had begun to change, and I could see it was my choice and my control. Much of what you will find in this plan will seem ridiculously simple at first, and you might be skeptical of its worth. It is my tried and true experience that I offer to you as testimonial. I began with very short steps, over and over again. When these simple steps became a habit, they really made an impact. All of this will be hard work, but the benefits will be amazing. You are worth it. As I write this plan, I admit that I am at about 85 percent capacity. It is similar to trying to lose those last 15 pounds of weight. I appreciate the 85 percent and don't ever plan to give it back. The last 15 percent may or may not happen, but my life is a constant stream of wonder and small miracles now that I have the focus to be aware of them.

CHAPTER SEVEN

We all have stressors in our lives that we really cannot do anything about. There are many stressors that we try to deal with, but in reality, we can eliminate them if we choose to do so. Choice plays a huge part in my plan. Over time I began to realize just how much choice I had in how my life, days, minutes went. The first steps were easy. I cancelled my newspapers. I didn't need to live the stresses of the entire world. I felt that if there was something I needed to know, someone would tell me. Ordinarily, I would wake up, get my newspapers, watch the early morning news shows while reading the papers, and drink a cup of tea. This routine was immediately eliminated from my life. I stopped watching any news shows and kept my mornings as quiet times of the day. This freed up at least an hour to do something positive to set the tone for the day. This was an extremely radical change, but took very little effort to initiate. I was pleasantly surprised how easy it was for me to give up the news. I began to feel less stressed almost immediately. I was not a big television viewer, but I did notice that when I watched in the evening with my husband, the shows tended to be of violence and drama. Well, I live enough drama in my daily life, with the addiction problems and fears, that I decided to eliminate any TV that had drama. This, of course, was most TV. This also gave me more free time to do other things.

Although my next step was a bit more radical and difficult to accomplish, I decided it was a necessary step. I began to slowly cut down my alignments with people, peripheral ones at first, who I did not enjoy being around and caused stress in my life. (Yes, it would have been great to eliminate the most stressful people in my life, but that was not possible; they are the ones I love the most.) As you saw in my story, I eventually had to eliminate my son from my home.

All of this I began slowly. Most of the "tools" I used in my plan, I began to use slowly. This will be a theme throughout. This new way of life could have been overwhelming if I hadn't done everything "small" at the beginning. The key to all of the tools I finally settled on using to implement my plan was consistency. Once I chose a tool, I used it, even if just for a few minutes each day, and it eventually became a habit. Each step I took, no matter how small and insignificant it seemed at the time, added to my sanity and serenity. As time progressed I was able to put minutes, and eventually hours, together of peace while living in the midst of chaos. At this point you might be thinking that free time is not exactly a good thing. Fears and anxieties have a chance to invade "free space" in your brain, which is disastrous. After the elimination process, whatever fits into your realm of unnecessary stresses, it is time to begin filling the time with small, at first, rewards.

CHAPTER EIGHT

I needed to begin to be around people again. I needed to be around people who I chose to be around. My life was full of my fearful and anxious family members, acquaintances and coworkers not privy to the situation, and those friends and family members with advice and judgment. Even people who I considered my friends had advice and an air of judgment that was sometimes unbearable. I didn't like the pity part, either. This is where the local support group came into play. During my extensive research, I read about these local family groups. Although I didn't need to be somewhere any more depressing and negative than I already was, I was desperate. I was pleasantly surprised. I attended my first meeting. I listened and watched and was not expected to participate. I did not participate. I considered that first meeting my first "reward" for attempting to improve my situation. As the hour progressed I noticed some joking and laughter among the attendees and wondered if, indeed, I was in the right place. Then I heard their stories and realized that all of these people lived my story, most of them longer and even more tragic. There were tales of visiting jails, hospitals, deaths, raising grandchildren because of addiction, and on and on. There was no one there to judge me and blame any of this on me. There was no advice, just experience. Indeed, they were all there for the same purpose, to reclaim their lives despite the chaos around.

This particular group was a 12-step program, very popular in the recovery field these days. Although I am not particularly taken by the structure and rigidity of some of these programs, I do what they suggest, and it works fine for me. The suggestion is to "take what you want and leave the rest." For me, in the early months of attending these meetings, I literally went for an escape from my reality to listen to others' worse realities. It was a relief to be somewhere for an hour a week where some- one wasn't judging me for being a bad mom or not doing what I should be doing (whatever that was) for my son. It gave me hope to see some of these people seemingly at peace in varying degrees and with hope. I recommend trying these groups, but can tell you they are not all the same, and they are not for everyone. There were not very many choices of where to go for help, and these meet- ings are free and nonthreatening. It is a good place to start. (See reference pages for finding meetings in your local area.)

CHAPTER NINE

Now it was time to fill in the "free" time with positive and valuable moments. My priority was really relaxing my body and my brain. Most of my research indicated that my best option was some kind of meditation or hypnosis program. I honed in on a few simple meditation formats and very slowly tried and practiced them. My intent was not spirituality (although I was certainly not against that) but something much more simple, just learning to empty out my mind. Whatever happened to enter my mind to take over the empty space was not my concern at this time. No thinking, giving my mind a rest, leading to resting my tense body, was really my only goal at this time. So, I began with the walking meditation I mentioned previously. Even that was a bit too complicated for me at the time. I tried the very basic meditation that most people begin with, following my breath. I tried to focus on breathing in one then out, in two then out, etc. This is how bad my focus was. I couldn't even get through a minute of this without having to begin again numerous times! I did persevere and, after lots of "do-overs," I slowly began to get it.

Along with the simple breathing, I found something that, for me, worked even better. I watched my dog while she was resting next to me and followed her breath. It required more focus because unlike my own breathing, I couldn't anticipate her breaths; I really had to pay attention to the rise and fall of her chest. Her breaths were not always regular, especially when she was having "puppy dreams," and this became one of my more popular mind-emptying meditations.

Another meditation (or focus exercise) was something I found relaxed me. I lit a small candle, with or without scent, and just watched the flame, focusing on its dancing rhythm and uneven movements. I tried to watch it for about half a minute. Then I would close my eyes and "see" how long I could keep the vision of the flame dancing in my mind's eye. This took lots of practice but was also fun, almost like a game.

A skill I worked on for a long time, beginning very slowly and building up time, is one of my best acquired methods of meditations and mentally escaping from a bad situation. It is probably a bit more self-hypnosis than meditation, but I highly recommend it to everyone. Initially, you'll need to practice this in a quiet place with no distractions, but after lots of practice, it won't matter where you are or how quiet it is, because in your mind you will be in a quiet place with no distractions. This might sound impossible and ridiculous to you. It did to me, initially, also. Truthfully, I don't really remember the exact way this was taught to me, so you are going to get my version.

Lie down or sit in a relaxing position in a quiet place with no distraction. Close your eyes. Think about a place where you would like to be, where you can be safe, protected from all the chaos around you, and you can really feel well-being. Begin listing in your mind all of the details of the place (colors, smells, air temperature, sounds, etc.) and then list, in detail, how you feel in this place. The more detailed your lists the better this exercise works. You are focusing on only good things and emptying your mind of negativity. In the beginning it will take you awhile to settle in to where you want to be and to focus on the details. Do this for as long as you can, probably only a few minutes at a time in the beginning. Eventually—it took me many months, actually—you will find that you are able to get yourself to this place almost immediately and feel the good feelings you have there. As you become adept at this, it will be something to use as a tool when otherwise you would be ready to explode about another crisis. In fact, I can sometimes get myself to my "place" in my mind while I'm talking to someone or actively trying to deal outwardly with a problem. I can literally "step back" in my mind without anyone around me knowing how disengaged I am. This comes in handy often during instigation and manipulation attempts of our active addicted loved ones. It is a wonderful skill to be used in many life situations. Remember, here again, practice, and it can eventually become a habit.

A variation of the above exercise, somewhat shorter, but can be as effective, is another good thing to do in the middle of a crisis situation. Again, begin to learn this in a quiet place with no distraction with your eyes closed. Think about a time and place that was so amazing you can feel the feeling you had quite intensely as soon as you think about it. There are a few different things I use here. I will give you an example of what I use, and I think you will get what the goal is here. To me, the most intense positive emotions I have ever felt were the two instances when the doctors put my newborn boys into my arms. It is emotion I can never forget and draw on often to escape from bad stress hormones overtaking my body. I could feel the excitement and joy pouring over and from within my entire body and surroundings, and nothing could change the emotion. It was so intense, I'll never forget how it felt, and in using this tool often, I am able to spend a lot of time feeling joyous and grateful. The important thing to remember is that our goal is to reduce stress and relax our bodies and minds. We need to be able to be centered so when everyone around us is enveloped in chaos, someone will be alert and able to act in an appropriate and levelheaded manner. It is important to be capable of focusing on the situation and ignoring the distractions. This practice will prepare us for that.

As you use these focus exercises on a regular basis, even a few moments each day, you will find that you are putting more minutes of calm together each day. Even a few minutes to begin the program will make a difference. Just to release your mind and body from constant tension, giving them a break, even short breaks, can make a difference in your health. As you practice some of these exercises, you'll find yourself making others up on your own to fit your lifestyle and schedule. I remember once I was sitting in the car in line at the bank drive-thru when a fly started walking on my side view mirror. I chose that time to focus on the fly, all the details. My focus was getting better, and I was able to see more details each day and extend my time not focused on chaos. I noticed how the fly had a kind of pattern across his body. His walk was rhythmic, and his eyes moved in a very strange way. After time it became a game to me. Before I began using my tools and trying to keep my sanity, this drive-thru line would have been a true disaster. Idle time would have netted me tense muscles, anxious thoughts, fears of things that probably would never happen, and I'm sure unnecessary rudeness when I got to the window. Saved by the fly!

If you can remember to grab a few moments here and there during the day during a busy schedule just to focus on good things or to empty the bad things, you will see your life change. It is easy to find these moments, but you must remember to do it. While at a stoplight, while driving, it is just the perfect amount of time to study the clouds or raindrops, or the person in the car next to you. Remember details! If you become really focused, a bit of a honk from behind will get you on your way. We do a lot of waiting for things in our daily lives. Use this time as opportunities for quick and simple meditations instead of challenges.

As I took time to focus on ordinary things, I began to realize just how extraordinary many things are. Do you know just how many different kinds of butterflies pass you by on a given spring day? There are so many different patterns on their beautiful wings! Have you ever really watched how skillful birds are at getting those bugs out of the ground for their food? Have you ever really taken time to watch those birds take off, fly, and land, and wonder how they do that? Do you ever take time to wonder about things like what is really going on in that dirt under that layer of grass? How many living things are under there, and what do they do all day? Why do the clouds look so fluffy?

As I was doing my research, I would read what people wrote; for instance, meditation is good for relaxing and focus. Also, there were examples of methods to use. As I have mentioned repeatedly in this book, as a mother of an addict I began to lose my ability to focus and do anything in depth. Not only was I unable to read a simple novel and remember what I read, I was barely able to read an entire magazine article unless it was on one page. So, what I wanted to see in all of this research were exact examples of instances where people could use these skills in their daily lives. I wanted to see how relevant they were to my life, loving addicts and alcoholics. For many reasons, although there are hundreds, probably thousands, of similar helpful books written, many people who love addicts believe they are different. It is different than coping with a sick or dying loved one. It is different than coping with our own illnesses. It is different than coping with mental illness, our own or our loved one's. Added to the anxiety and fears related to these problems, there are the elements of choice, blame, criminal activity, aggression, and manipulation just to name a few. I will do my best to integrate these tools with personal experiences.

The following is a perfect example of being able to draw from my meditation practice to improve my situation during a major crisis.

After my son had spent almost 90 days in the long-term rehab facility out west (3,000 miles away from our home), I received a phone call early one morning from the director of the facility. This would be the third time my son had been in a rehab program, so at this point I was being cautiously optimistic about the value of rehabilitation programs. She very calmly advised me that my 20-year-old son had left the facility in the middle of the night with a new resident. Their policy was that if a resident left on his own before the agreed time, he was not allowed back at the facility. She informed me that he was not welcome to return even if he wished to. When I asked her to evaluate the situation, she said that the man my son left with could possibly be dangerous. She referred to him as a "gang-banger," which didn't mean much to me at the time since it was not part of my vocabulary. When I asked if it was possible that my son might be dead on the side of the highway somewhere, she did not rule it out. So, nobody knew where my son was and expected that he could possibly be in danger, and there was no way to reach him. As most of us related to addicts know, this all is really not that unusual. Scary, isn't it?

My husband and older son happened to be home at the time of the call. After I relayed the information to them, it was time for panic to set in. This is where my "training" came in to play. This was the perfect time for chaos, fear, anxiety, and panic. Instead, I left my family to their own insecurities and excused myself for a few minutes. Before the muscles began to tense, the headache began, and the stress hormones ran rampant, I stepped back into a quiet place, took a few deep breaths, and did one of my meditations for about ten minutes, keeping my mind completely empty of anything. I did not strategize, scream, overthink; I just was. I think my family thought I had actually lost my mind. Little did they know I was actually finding it. When I finished my meditation I felt calm and clearheaded. I evaluated the situation and decided to call the director back and get more details and ask about my options. She reiterated that it was against their policy to take him back, and she gave me names of two other facilities that he might be able to get into if he still wanted recovery. Needless to say, it could have been one of the worst days of my life, yet it turned out to be quite interesting and a true testimonial to the value of the work I had been doing on myself. Without going into the crazy details of the day, I'll tell you that I believe that being calm and levelheaded that day was crucial to the future of my son's recovery.

After a very long day the result was a true miracle. By midnight, my son was welcomed back into the current facility, although they had never gone against policy before, and he continued there for another four months. Yes, he had used, relapsed the night he left, and he had put himself into a very dangerous situation, but after a chain of almost unbelievable events (my participation was a link in this chain of events), he has been clean and sober since that night, almost four years ago. I would like to emphasize here that a very small thing, such as a ten-minute meditation, played a big part in this scenario. Each small step forward adds up.

In the reference section later on in this book, chapter thirteen, you will find some books on meditation that I found useful and still refer to for new ideas. They are simple but powerful.

CHAPTER TEN

The tools in this section are obvious for those who are not distracted by chaos. This is more of a reminder that we need to get back to doing some things for ourselves rather than being dedicated to only doing things for others. Taking care of ourselves can make us better people.

SOAK – After living in the same house for over ten years and after an especially tenuous day living with an addict, I decided to put some water in the tub I had never used, add some bubble bath and some oil, light a few small candles, and turn off the lights. Again, I soaked in that tub, meditated on the flickering of the candles, and momentarily forgot the fears of the outside world. This became another habit that I feel sometimes saved my sanity. At times I added some favorite calming music to the mix. It was like a mini vacation away from it all. This is another way to grab a few minutes of sanity. Yes, chaos is still waiting for you, but stealing a few minutes away from it can do wonderful things to break the tension in your body and mind.

WALK – I like to walk. We all know that getting oxygen to the brain and, for that matter, throughout the body keeps us alert and healthy. While I was addicted to my addict and had no other focus, I stopped exercising and walking. When I decided to begin this program, I was afraid my walking would just give my brain too much idle time again and make me more crazy. So, I went to the library and downloaded some interesting motivational and inspirational books onto my MP3 player and listened to them while I walked. This was another positive way of distracting me from the chaos in my life while adding other tools to use to increase my well-being. I often listened to music with only positive messages, usually music that brought back memories of good times. Whatever I did, I did not allow walking in silence, which would allow the fears and anxieties to enter my mind. Walking can be time consuming, but being creative can fit it into our daily activities. Also, remember the walking meditation. If I was just walking from place to place, maybe running errands, I would count my steps to fill up that empty space so the thoughts of chaos were blocked out. Some of the books I found especially helpful are listed in my reference section.

MUSIC – Let's talk about music. I began to listen to music, but only a certain kind. Everyone has their own personal taste in music, but I found that music with harsh, negative messages (even if they did happen to have a snappy tune) needed to be eliminated, just like the news. For me, it was helpful to find music, even music that I wouldn't normally be interested in, that touched on the subject of good relationships, especially at the time, good relationships with moms and sons. For instance, I happened upon a Celine Dion album called *Miracle*. It is dedicated to her relationship with her young son. I've really never been a fan of this singer and don't own any other album of hers. But this particular album touched me because I was so desperate for those times in the past when my son and I were so close. I enjoyed hearing the music, just knowing that the more I felt those good feelings of our past good relationship, I could almost will them to return. I have heard from some other parents that it hurt them to hear this kind of music because they missed those relationships so much and what their children used to be. I guess everyone is different. It gave me hope. Somehow it confirmed to me that somewhere in that ravaged, drug-addicted brain and body, that sweet little boy was still there to be rediscovered. The music was therapy for me. I listened to "fun" music whenever I could. I have a little convertible. I live in Florida so I can have the top down almost all of the time. It was another way to escape, with the upbeat music blaring and the wind blowing in my face. I always tried to focus on the music and driving, and leave the chaos for another time. So, walking, driving, soaking in the tub, these are more sane moments I chose to add to my plan. Just as a reminder, choice is a key factor here.

GRATITUDE – Addiction can and does take over the lives of entire families. It can often seem that the whole world is against us and we are alone in our fears and anxieties. We can only see the destruction of a life and a family, and it becomes overwhelming. It is important to not lose sight of reality. Yes, there is chaos around, but the good things in our lives are still there. They have not disappeared. Everyone has much to be grateful for. Until I remembered this I was lost. It was suggested to me that I remember the good things in life, too. So, I made a plan, a very simple plan, for starting my days. Since I was touched by this pain of addiction, it was difficult to even get up in the mornings. Of course, I didn't sleep very well, so I was always very tired. When I woke in the morning, my first thoughts were of what horrible things would occur that day. Will my son be alive? Will he be put in jail? Will we argue? How will today's manipulation play out? This was what set the tone for my days. So, with my new plan I decided to make a new choice. Each morning, even before I get out of bed, I focus on and choose five things to be grateful for. For instance, I am often simply grateful for my hot cup of tea in the morning. I think about the taste, the smell, the feel of the warm cup, and how relaxed I feel when I am drinking it. After choosing five different things and really focusing on them, my day ends up starting out on a positive note. This, also, is simple to do, takes little time, and costs nothing. Another few minutes of calm. This will take practice but, after repetition, will become a habit you will appreciate.

FLOAT – I am lucky enough to have a pool at my home and can use it every day. Most people I know do not ever get into their pools. Mine is therapy for me.

There, again, I choose my music carefully, walk or swim, end up with some floating and watching the clouds and their curious formations.

GARDEN – All of my life, those who knew me well would never give me flowers as a gift. They knew that in a matter of a few hours or days at the most, the flowers would be dead. I truly had a black thumb. During my practice of putting minutes together of focus and turning them into hours of more disciplined focus, I noticed a small hibiscus bush in my side yard. It had been slowly leaning and was now lying on the ground, still rooted. My neighbor, who is an avid gardener, had mentioned to me numerous times that it would be a good thing to pay a bit of attention to the bush. She offered to help me upright it, but in my usual inattentive, black thumb way, I thanked her for her offer but chose not to do anything. A few days later, while I was out in the yard with the dog, my neighbor was, again, out in her garden and offered to help with the hibiscus bush. Mostly to appease her I went into the garage and got some sticks and rope, and together we put up the bush. Actually it was quite an accomplishment. I felt good and the dog was really happy, being able to spend an extended period of time outdoors that day. During the week, while I was out running some errands, I stopped and bought some plant food. Again, the pup and I went out and watered the bush and spread a bit of food. We began to check on it daily. After only a week or two, the browned and yellowed leaves began to turn a deep vibrant green. Buds began to pop out, and soon there were beautiful red

Denise Krochta

hibiscus flowers all over the bush. I thought about the bush in relationship to my transition to taking better care of myself. We were a lot alike. Just a little bit of nurturing and attention, and life was better! I soon went out and bought some dirt and a few more plants to see what I could do with them. I spent a little bit of time each day watering, pruning, and talking to them, and they eventually became a beautiful garden. The dog was happy spending time outside in the garden. Taking time each day to see the changes in the garden and appreciate the beauty of the flowers, butterflies, bees, etc. was indeed therapy for me. This became another escape from the chaos that surrounded me.

CHAPTER ELEVEN

WRITING

When I was a kid, someone, and I don't even remember who, told me not to write anything down unless I wanted to be reminded of it and regret it, taking the chance everyone and anyone could read it. So, even as a little girl I didn't keep a journal or a diary, and rarely wrote letters to anyone. I saved any writing for required papers at school. This was one of those things we do because somewhere in the back of our minds we vaguely remember a rule to live by but have no clue the roots of the rule.

Anyway, with little ability to focus but still having to run a family and business, I began to write down everything, just to give myself a chance of remembering things. I bought empty notebooks and used them for everything. I had one for the car to write down lists. I had one in the house for more lists. I wrote what I needed to be doing. I wrote what I had forgotten to do. I wrote lists to remind me to read my other lists. Yes, this was a crazy time. About this time, since I had all these empty notebooks, I decided to try some of the suggestions I had come across in my research. I had originally discarded the ideas because they had to do with writing things down, and my old rule told me this was a bad idea. Addiction brought to my attention that all rules can be broken, so I took the opportunity to go along with the current trend in my house, and broke this rule, too.

I began by starting a gratitude journal. Similar to my thoughts of gratitude I tried to wake up to each day, I wrote my thoughts down, either the same ones or different ones. I also found that when I was in the middle of a crisis or especially if I knew some really bad things were going on with my son that day, and expectations of bad things to come were weighing me down, I did a little writing exercise. I sat down and wrote down exactly how I was feeling. I wrote about what I thought was going to happen, why I worried about it, what I thought I should do about it, and what I could do for me to make it better. For me, just putting this down on paper actually made it feel a step away from me, not inside of me. It was like having a therapist to listen to you. I got it off my chest, and it just was a bit less fearful. I did this very often and kept it all in a notebook.

Another very helpful writing tool was directly related to my reactions to my son and his anger and manipulation. At least once a week I sat down and wrote a letter to my son. I told him everything I was thinking about him at the time. I often told him how much I loved him, how sad I was because of him, how anxious and fearful I was for him and sometimes of him. Everything I wanted him to know I wrote in these letters. Then, after I got everything down just the way I wanted it, I ripped the letter into a million pieces and tossed it in the trash. You see, in his active addiction, I knew that he really didn't care how I felt; he couldn't, and if I saved these letters for his recovery, which I wished for every day, this guilt would not be something he would need and would not help his recovery. Again, it helped me to write everything down and sort out my thoughts. It just felt good, in a strange kind of way.

The very best and most helpful writing tool for my plan was this next one. I took an empty notebook, and each day I spent a few minutes basically dreaming. I sat and thought about something I wished would be true, mostly small things, sometimes big things, and wrote them down. Most of the wishes seemed impossible at the time, but I hoped they weren't unrealistic. For instance, I wrote one day that I hoped to see my two sons have a sibling relationship. Drug addicts in active addiction can't really have a relationship with anyone. But, I dreamed of a time where my sons, who are less than two years apart, could bond because they wanted to. I also wished for things as seemingly small as a genuine hello or good-bye from family members, including the addict. Our home had become quiet and tense when not explosive. What I learned from this exercise is this. If you write something down, it can help to make it real. If you wish for things but don't write them down, you might not remember in the future that you wished for this and it came true. Often, we think our wishes never come true and there are no small (or large) miracles. But as life happens we seem to forget. As I review the pages over two years of this past exercise, it is impossible to not feel blessed with more than I could ever have imagined. To actually see and understand some of these perceived impossible things come true certainly can light up a seemingly terrible life. Writing can help us to become more aware.

CHAPTER TWELVE

I am not a therapist. I am not a doctor. I am not a recovering addict who became a therapist. In fact, I am probably more "clean" when it comes to smoking, drinking, drugs, and experimenting than anyone you will meet who grew up in the sixties and seventies. I am just a mom who tried to do the best possible when raising her family. This chapter is full of my observations from my experiences. This is not resulting from scientific or psychological experimental data. I believe that experience is a very valuable teacher, and I offer this experience for you to consider in your planning and strategizing through this episode in your lives.

REACTING – One thing all addicts are very good at is manipulation. They like to get immediate reactions from their loved ones. If we can step back, take a few deep breaths, and either don't react or keep reactions minimal, this throws them off course. After doing this for a while with my son, things in the house became more calm. If he couldn't get an immediate reaction and rile me up, it just wasn't worth it to him to try. Too much work. While this made his life a bit more difficult, it helped me to keep my blood pressure from rising, my muscles could stay relaxed, and he would do what he was going to do, anyway.

REASONING – I would like to encourage you to read the book on my reference pages by Abraham Twerski, MD. It is called *Addictive Thinking (Understanding Self-Deception)*. It is an excellent, short book about addictive thinking. It convinced me that trying to reason with an addict was, indeed, an act of futility. This book, along with some of the information on the free Web sites I have listed about how the addicted brain works, I hope will convince you also. After coming to understand about this thought process, it was easier for me not to take things personally, and also to know that what they were arguing about and lying about were actually, in their minds, the truth. Simply put, if someone really believes that two plus two is five, then no amount of reasoning is going to change his mind. You are wrong, an idiot. He is right. Knowing this information often calmed my mind and my body. This was big for me. You cannot reason with an addict! Trying is another stressful act.

TAKING THINGS PERSONALLY – Addicts are most angry with and abusive to those they love the most. My son really loved me! As I learned that his brain was really hijacked by these drugs and it was almost impossible for him to make good judgments, reason, and make decisions, I understood that it was really a physical and mental illness, not a matter of love that he acted like he did. As I took less of this personally, that relieved my stress also. It is important to remember, an addict's body and mind crave these drugs as soon as they have none in their systems, sometimes before. The only goal in their minds is where will the next "fix" come from. You are only in their way. They can't feel anything for you. It has nothing to do with willpower. They would love us if they could.

BLAME – We dig down deep to discover who is to blame for these addictions. Someone must be to blame. What I have learned is this. Even if there is a clear-cut, obvious place to put blame, it is not useful. If we spend time blaming, we are using precious time in a negative way. Blame is the past and we must focus on the present. I don't think that those who cannot leave the past behind can really ever recover. Maybe they will stop their bad habits and rehabilitate from their addictions, but if they can't let go of blame, then they are not free to "soar" into a positive future.

Blame doesn't accomplish anything and is a major roadblock. I know that many therapists believe that they must get to the root of the problems, and blame plays a big part in that therapy. To me, it seems to give the addict just another reason not to take responsibility for his life. This cannot help with progress. When it comes to addiction, I think sometimes it just happens. Genetics, perceptions, peer pressure, abuse, environment all play a part. It is like the rest of life. We must do the best we can. We cannot always be second-guessing this. Just like we know there probably won't be a cure for addiction in our lifetime, we know that there are millions of reasons why this could happen to our loved ones. We are not going to get rid of the chaos, so let's work on living with it.

WORRY – We are all very good at this. I learned that all the worrying I did in my early days of dealing with addiction was for naught. The only thing worrying does is tense up those muscles, hike up that blood pressure, increase those headaches, and ruin your day. It does none of these things for the addict. Usually, they are out in oblivion. The fact that most of what we worry about never happens is probably true. Just think of all the time we spend doing it. Because we know that most causes of our worry are things we can do nothing about, I decided to try a new rule. Don't worry until you know you must. Judging this was difficult at first, but with time, I got to know when it really was necessary. I was driving over the bridge from our town to the adjacent town recently and I saw this sign. "Decide not to worry for two days. Today and Tomorrow." Think about it.

PERCEPTIONS – What goes on in the minds of these addicts? Do we really know what goes on in anybody's mind? Even in a healthy mind perceptions can be different. I have an identical twin sister. When we talk about our youth the stories always amaze me. We lived in the same house, shared a bedroom, at the exact same time, with the same family, virtually doing most of the same things, especially when we were really young. When we relate stories, many times the details are all different. Sometimes some of the main events are portrayed completely different. So, when we add distortion through drugs and alcohol we can see how difficult it is to really know why things happen. Many times addicts are working off major misperceptions to keep them in their downward spiral. There is no way for us to know because chances are we are looking for different things. We can only try to control our own thoughts and be content with our perceptions.

ENABLING – This word simply means to give someone the means to do something. Many of our well-meaning actions actually give our addicts the means to continue making bad choices. We sit in sadness and fear while walking on eggshells. We do this while we are giving them money, not requiring them to meet any responsibilities, many times making life easy enough for them to let us do all of the worrying and work so they can be free to continue their habits. We all want to save them from their possible, even probable, plight (jail, illness, death, losing jobs, etc.).

I remember standing in long lines at motor vehicle bureaus throughout our state to try to pay fines and save my son from losing his driver's license. He eventually lost his license because he chose not to take an eight-hour course that would have helped him keep his license. I made excuses for him when he was surly with my friends and others. I gave him money when he should have been making his own. He has always been a smart, able-bodied young man. When I bought a new car, I gave him my previous car to use at college. I paid the insurance on this car and paid for maintenance, and even for gas. He really had no responsibility. I wanted him to focus on college. We paid for his apartment; dorm life wasn't his cup of tea. So, he had free time for using, dealing, driving while using, putting miles on the car requiring more maintenance, gas, etc. Needless to say, college wasn't his priority. So, although I felt guilty and worried about him feeling unloved, as well as being judged by all of my critics, I began to stop the enabling. I realized that it was making me resentful and even hateful of the situation and even of my son. I took the car away. What a relief! Yes, he was angry, mean, manipulative, and full of blame. But, truthfully, not having to worry he was out driving and possibly killing himself and other helpless victims with my car lessened my stress. When he needed rides, if I was available and didn't need to go out of my way, I would drive him. If not, he had to find his own rides. This all conveniently coincided with the revocation of his driver's license. When he got it back, we just did not return the car to him. This all made it a bit more difficult for him to carry on his habits. He had to work harder.

I stopped following him around to confirm that he was at school or at recovery meetings, or not meeting drug dealers. I stopped going through his room each time he left the house. I knew what I would find, anyway, and what he would deny. I stopped giving him cash. If there were school books to pay for or what I knew were legitimate expenses that I didn't mind paying for, the money went right to the source, not through him. We want to take care of our loved ones and think we are doing the best for them when we help them. Many addicts are in this position because of low self-esteem. I read many times in my research about this. It is explained that when we continuously do things for our addicts, it often convinces them that they aren't capable and are judged by us to be incompetent and less able. They don't get to feel a sense of accomplishment by doing something on their own, and this just encourages this feeling of low self-worth. I don't know if I completely believe this, although I can tell you how confident my son seems now that he is clean, sober, and responsible for his own life. He is the only judge he really cares about. His harshest critic, I'm sure, but he is fine with that. When dealing with grown men and women with families, jobs, and financial responsibilities, enabling comes into play even more. From my experience, we all need to learn more about ourselves and define our priorities. If we have children, we have to consider their safety and sometimes make life-changing moves. When spouses lose jobs, are incarcerated, deplete the family of funds, the dynamics are different, but the basic, underlying problem is the same. Anger and manipulation may come in different packages, but they are still anger and manipulation. Dead is dead, when it comes right down to it. Aren't all lives equal? I remember someone saying that it is different when it is your child who is the addict. We can divorce a spouse, remove ourselves from a sibling or abusive parent. In my opinion, all relationships have their unique and distinguishing anxieties and fears, but when it comes right down to it, the basic premise of this book is the key. We must take care of ourselves and learn how to choose peace, serenity, and joy while in the midst of chaos. When I stopped most of my enabling habits I made for myself another unspoken rule. I would only do things that I could be comfortable with. If I resented what I was doing, I just said no. As I followed this practice, it became easier to say no and less stressful. I thought what I had been doing was love. It was enabling. There are books on enabling in the libraries and bookstores. Check my reference page for where to start.

REHABS AND THERAPY FOR ADDICTS – Addiction is a scary thing. There are not many answers, and treatments vary. For the addict, rehab and therapy or 12-step programs are mostly what is available at this time. It is difficult to make a decision both for the loved ones and the addict with regards to a plan. The majority of rehabilitation facilities are cost prohibitive to most people. We spent enough money to buy a very nice house. We were fortunate to have access to funds to provide this for our son. Only a small percentage of those afflicted with this disease have these kind of resources. (Search the Web sites on the reference page for possible scholarships.) Addiction is a solitary disease. The 12-step programs for addicts provide a place to go to learn a sober lifestyle in a group setting. Ideally, an addict will go to a long-term rehab program and continue with a 12-step group when he finishes the program. Long-term rehab makes more sense to me. According to the experts, it takes at least 30 to 45 days of sobriety for a person's brain to be clear enough to even make decisions about recovery. Most rehab programs are only 30-day programs. The statistics show that the longer one is in rehab the better the chance of long-term recovery. Isolation is not a good thing. Becoming part of a supportive group after rehab is also an indication of a possible long-term recovery.

There is information about rehabs and therapy on the Web sites listed on the reference pages in chapter thirteen.

SECRETS – You will find that this is not a subject people like to share with others. You will probably not want to share this with others. Yes, there will be judgment, condemnation, advice, pity. BUT, secrets can make you sick. Attending the support groups will help with this. Talking about this problem with others who have lived it will help. Keeping this secret from your family, friends, employees, and employers can be extremely stressful. Living among people who have no idea about your pain can often be unbearable. This is what I learned from my experience. When I decided that I would no longer be embarrassed and self-critical about having this in my family, I began to share with others. To my surprise at the time (not anymore) the majority of people I opened up to about this had their own stories about addiction in their families. Most of them had never shared this with anyone. It was their secret. Being able to speak with someone and share their pain without judgment or condemnation freed them of some of their pain. I heard stories of brothers in jail, people growing up with alcoholic parents, marriages broken by this disease, etc. According to my research, one out of four families is touched by addiction in some way, and each addiction touches one hundred people in their lives. These are very general, nonscientific statistics, but just in my own experience, I can see how they can be true. My point here is that a lot of people are keeping this secret for fear of being judged or pitied, putting unnecessary stress on those who have enough stress trying to live with this problem. I believe that there would be a lot more people helping each other through this if it weren't such a secret. This, again, is another choice to make. Do you want to live with the added stress of secrecy?

THERAPY FOR LOVED ONES – For those who have unlimited funds I hear that lots of therapy is helpful. It was not something I was able to do, so I can't personally recommend it. I think it could be helpful.

PRAYER – For those who are inclined, prayer is certainly a good addition to any positive program. I once heard it said that "prayer is talking to God, and meditation is listening to God." I like this and find it comforting.

CHAPTER THIRTEEN

REFERENCES

I am keeping this simple. The Web sites listed below will lead you to more information than you'll ever want to know. They are what I found to be the most current information available.

The books, Web sites, and DVDs on this list are part of the core foundation of this plan. There are many other books in the library, bookstores, and online related to these subjects. I list these books because they are short, concise, and can give you immediate useful information and results.

www.hbo.com/addiction
www.samhsa.gov
www.dasis3.samhsa.gov
www.drugabuse.gov
www.nar-anon.org
www.alanon.org

Books and DVDs

Addictive Thinking (Understanding Self-Deception) second edition, by Abraham J. Twerski, MD

The Three Minute Meditator (Reduce Stress. Control Fear. Diminish Anger in Almost No Time At All. Anywhere. Anytime.), by David Harp, MA and Nina Smiley, PhD

Practicing the Power of Now, by Eckhart Tolle

HBO Addiction, Why Can't They Just Stop (This book is to accompany the DVDs produced for the special shown on HBO in April of 2007. It can be purchased along with the DVDs on the Web site mentioned above. The DVDs can be viewed free on that Web site and also found in some libraries.)

HBO DVD series *Addiction*

Spirituality

Illuminata, by Marianne Williamson

10 Secrets for Success and Inner Peace, by Dr. Wayne Dyer

Change Your Thoughts—Change Your Life, by Dr. Wayne Dyer

PART THREE

WALKING THE WALK

"Experience is not what happens to you, it is what you do with what happens to you."
- Aldous Huxley

CHAPTER FOURTEEN

It was dusk, and we were just getting off the high-way. There was a dirt road up ahead with a sign to the Indian reservation. I was driving, and my 21-year-old son was navigating. As we followed the narrow road over bumps and holes, trying to do minimal damage to my rental car, I wondered what I was getting myself into. I wondered how my son had found these new friends and how they were related to his recovery process. I hoped this would be another opportunity for us to get close and to heal some past "wounds."

It was beginning to mist, almost a drizzle, and the dust started to mat down on the car. My son told me to slow down; we were approaching the right turn into the driveway. Others began to arrive. There were already a few trucks in the driveway ahead of us. Although there was a chill in the air and the threat of rain loomed in the sky, we got out of the car dressed in shorts and bathing suits under our sweats. We grabbed a couple of gallon jugs of water from the back of the car and headed down the path. There were already about eight Native Ameri-can men chatting with each other and stoking the fire. They were gathering the sage and other sacred herbs, the drum, the flute, the rattles, and other tools for the evening. There were many rocks heating up in the fire for later.

The men, young and old, welcomed my son and me with opened arms. At this point I was the only woman there. One of the guys was a very good friend of my son's, and he introduced us to the others. As we visited, more men came. Most of the men were Native Americans and knew each other. They all were very warm and welcoming to us. We were introduced to the "leader" of the group. He was dressed in black swimming trunks with no shirt. He was a short, stocky guy. His rather rotund belly hung over his bathing suit. I guess, to me, he was more Santa Claus on summer vacation than "chief" like. His hair was pulled back into a short ponytail. The smile on his broad face was warm enough to melt an ice-cream cone on the spot. Two mutts who lived on the reservation also took their opportunity to welcome us. They were kind of dirty and smelly but, like everyone else, seemed happy and relaxed.

My son told me to keep drinking water while I was standing around. As the people continued to arrive, I stepped back and watched what was going on. One of the men continued to stoke the fire, and it was very hot. By now the night was dark, and in the flickering of the fire, I could see the star of the evening: the sweat lodge. It was a dome-shaped structure covered with thick canvas, like a tarp. It was only about 10 to 15 feet in diameter. The door, a flap of the canvas, was open, and I could see inside. In the middle of the lodge was a sunken fire pit. Around the fire pit was an earthen bench also sunken in the ground. I noticed it was all very dark, damp, and musty. The ceiling was only about six feet high. I looked up into the sky and noticed the clouds rolling in, a preface to the predicted storm no doubt, but there was no rain.

What the heck was going on, and why was I there? These are excellent questions, ones that I had asked myself about a million times up to that point. My son, who lives out West, had told me about this awe-inspiring experience he had had a few times with some of his new Native American friends. At the time, I was visiting him from Florida to support him on his celebration of his first full year of being drug and alcohol free. The prior years were so destructive and horrific, I was anxious to celebrate this wonderful and positive time with him.

So, one of the things he was doing during the week was to participate in a Native American Sweat Ceremony. When he described it to me after he had first participated in one, I put it on my list as something I would never be able to do. He said that he always had a really good feeling after the ceremony. I wasn't really expecting that for myself.

Ever since I was born, I have been afflicted with major claustrophobia. I know I have missed out on many things in my life because of this, but nothing I have tried has relieved this problem. I believe that when my twin sister and I were still in my mother's womb, we were situated in a way where she got most of the oxygen and nutrients from the placenta, and I got only what was left. When we were born, she was a healthy, large, robust baby, and I was very underweight and had to stay in the hospital for two weeks. Anyway, that is my theory of why I have this problem. Suffice it to say, sometimes this claustrophobia runs my life, and it is not a good thing. For instance, once I woke my husband up in the middle of the night and forced him to cut off my wedding ring because I couldn't get it off, and I couldn't breathe! Another time I was in the mountains, out in the open air at night, but there were no lights, the darkness was suffocating, and I panicked because I couldn't breathe. There were many times when I missed out on wonderful experiences because of this problem. When I was a teen, I went to Babi Yar, in the Ukraine, to the tombs, and instead of seeing and learning the history of what happened there, I literally walked through the narrow passage with my eyes closed, in pure panic. When my family went tubing in a cave in Belize, I didn't even bother trying it. Of course, they said it was wonderful. I've missed many stalactites and stalagmites in caves all over the world due to pure panic. Anyway, I think you get the picture. It is not just closed spaces; this is a problem way beyond that.

During my visit that week, I told my son I was there to support him, and I was willing to do anything to support his celebration. So, there I was, about to get into a dark, hot, closed-in hut with 14 sweaty strangers. Was I a bit anxious? I brought some music and a book in case I had to wait in the car for my son. I came with little confidence in myself.

One of the young men picked up some dried sage and lit it. It began to smoke. He waved it around his whole body, a purifying procedure, a kind of blessing, before going into the hut. I had seen this done earlier in the week at another Native American gathering I attended. He offered the burning sage to me, and I mimicked what he had done. It occurred to me that I needed all the help I could get, so I gladly added this step.

Just before it was time to enter the hut, another woman arrived. She turned out to be the wife of the keeper of the sweat lodge and reservation. She had participated numerous times in these ceremonies and looked excited, not crazed like me.

It is tradition that the leader enters the lodge first and then the women. The leader had been sitting for a minute or two when he called for the two of us to enter. As we stepped into the hut, we were to turn to the left, walk all around the fire pit, and sit next to him, near the door. The men came in. My son had informed me earlier that one of the times he did this there were only four people. This time it was packed tight, and I mean tight! There were 15 of us in this tiny hut! My anxiety was already beginning to start when the door was still open, and they had not yet begun to bring the hot rocks. One of the guys from outside brought in these large, hot, glowing rocks, one by one. As he deposited each, one at a time, at the feet of the leader, he, in turn, lifted the rock with these tools, which looked like little antlers, and deposited them in the fire pit. As he put more and more rocks in, the hut became warmer. After about 15 rocks were put in and just about filled the pit, they stopped bringing the rocks, and he said it was time. The door was shut! What did I get myself into this time! I sat next to the leader. He had earlier informed me that this was a difficult experience for many people, especially first timers. (And that would be for first timers without claustrophobia!) He told me there would be three parts, and after each "flap" (this refers to the closing of the door) there would be a short break. If I needed to leave at any time during the flap, before breaks, I just needed to let him know by saying "door," and they would pause and let me out. That was comforting. Well, not really!

As I said, they let down the door flap, and the ceremony began. As I understood it, a Sweat Ceremony is a spiritual experience where there are lots of songs, prayers, and offerings. It is a purification of the body, mind, and spirit. It is also a time for each participant to express prayers, desires, hopes, and gratitude to their creator. They throw sage and sacred herbs on the hot rocks and offer them, also. My heart was pounding, my throat was closing up, and I was sweating like a pig (of course, initially this was from my anxiety, long before the hot rocks came into play). I began to panic. It was very dark, but I could see my son across the hut from the glow of the rocks. I could tell he saw my panic and held little hope for me. What a dilemma! Whatever possessed me to even think I could do this! I looked at the woman next to me and whispered, "I think I'm already done." She smiled at me and suggested I try another minute or so. Not much help there!

At this time, the leader began to speak about the reason for the Sweat, the purification process, and the gratitude in his heart for the opportunity. He had a bucket of water next to him and threw some from a ladle onto the rocks. So, not only was it dark and hot; now it was steamy! I could feel my nostrils closing up and my heart beating even faster, thinking this was really going to be a disaster! All of a sudden, I heard the drum and the men starting to shout songs to the beat of the drum. They were praying in a Native American language, and it was inspiring (and distracting for the moment). As they sang, shook rattles, and beat the drum, the leader continued to throw ladles of water to make the steam. By this time, I knew they were going to have to carry me out of there, either from fainting, a coma, or death. There was just no more breathing to be done!

I never actually got the details of what they did in the hut, how long each "flap" would be, and what would happen during the break. So, at this point, I had probably been in the hut for a total of 15 minutes. My shirt and shorts dripped with sweat, mine and my neighbors'. I figured this first session should be over soon, so I was determined to make it through. I did many things to distract myself. I focused on the sentiments of the leader, which were quite moving. I began to sing along (faking it, of course) and to dance to the drum (using the term *dance* loosely, since we were packed tighter than sardines). I took a moment to mentally remove myself from my surroundings and reflect on all of the "tools" I had been putting in my "toolbox" over the past few years to deal with fear, panic, and chaos. I felt this was the perfect opportunity to try some of them, so I tried a few three- to four-minute meditations in the middle of all this. First, I just tried to follow my breath. Focusing on it gave me the confidence that I actually could breathe. Then, I was on my favorite Pacific beach, sitting on a rocky ledge with the cool salt air blowing in my face. I could almost hear the waves crashing against the rocks. I'm still not an expert at this meditation and focusing stuff, so this distraction didn't last too long. Of course, bottom line, I expected my false sense of security—that this first part would be over soon—would get me through.

As time passed, I began to really get into the ceremony itself, the stories and songs, the smell of the herbs, and I was beginning to breathe a bit again. There was a feeling of high, positive energy in the hut. Many of the prayers and sentiments focused on my son and his past torments and current success. They appreciated his gratitude for me being with him to celebrate. There were other members attending this Sweat from the local recovery community who understood how important this was. It is not unusual for friends and relatives to completely disown the addicts and alcoholics, no matter how long they have been clean and sober. Support is a "gift." The group was so kind with sentiments about mothers, their trials and deep love for their children, and about me in particular. It certainly was impossible to get up and leave in the midst of this! Finally, after about 45 minutes, the rocks cooled down, and the leader yelled to the "keepers of the fire" outside to open the door.

What a relief! The door was opened! The cold night air came into the hut, but nothing else happened. No one got up to go out; there was no water break. Believe me, there was lots of sweating going on, and water really would have been a good thing. The group chatted a bit, told a few jokes, then (oh my God!) here came more hot rocks! I didn't know what to do. I had planned on surviving the first "flap" no matter what, and I did. It was way more than I believed I could have done. I knew that if I was leaving, this was the time. The rocks, which were much hotter than the first batch since they were on the fire 45 minutes longer, were being piled up in the fire pit, and it was now time for the door to close. I did know that this second "flap" was very important. During this time, each person got the opportunity to offer up their prayers, gratitude, hopes, and individual sentiments in front of the group. Since I was the first one sitting next to the leader, I decided to stay in, give my offering (I felt I owed it to my son, and I really wanted to express how I felt from my heart and soul), and then yell, "Door" and get the heck out!

So, the hut was hotter than a sauna now, the sacred sage and herbs were thrown on the rocks, a prayer was sung, and it was time for the individual offerings. The leader explained that he would start and then they would go around the tent, one by one. When each person was done speaking, they were to end with the phrase "all my relations," and that is how the next person would know it was his or her turn to speak.

He spoke for about ten minutes. It was very moving, and because I knew I'd be out of there momentarily, I focused fully on him, felt the spirituality in the room, along with the love surrounding us all, and the presence of a higher energy. I was wholeheartedly inspired, now that I was fully focused! When he finished, I waited for him to say, "All my relations," but instead he said, "We will now begin on my left and go around the hut." *Panic!* I was seated on his right! I would be the 15th person to speak! I immediately began to calculate how long this would take if the average offering was only two minutes. I was looking at a minimum of a half hour more! And who knew if that's all they did in this flap! Could I do it? Could I last? The leader began to pour more water on the rocks, which were glowing like hot lava. The steam rose, nice and hot, and the sweat just poured out of every pore in my body. I began to consider my options. I could leave now and breathe. Or, I could see how it went for a while and then leave and breathe! Or, I could "be a man" and quit succumbing to my demons and "get with the program" and stay. I was leaning toward the first option, of course, when the first gentleman began. He spoke about honoring the elders, some recent experiences he had with friends, and his gratitude for having a youthful representation at this first Sweat of the Spring. He also acknowledged my son and his accomplishments. He then began to speak about mothers, too. He soon said, "All my relations" and was done. The next person began his offering, continuing the theme of mothers and their unconditional love, suffering because of the troubles of their children, etc. So how could I leave now? This woman beside me and I were the only mothers in the hut. It would be impossible to leave now! The leader continued to throw water on the rocks, which were very hot now. The steam rose, basically cementing my nostrils closed.

At this time, I was beginning to realize that my moments of panic were lessening, and I was becoming able to do some "mind over matter" work on myself. I began to notice the steady dripping of something on my left foot. It was the sweat pouring off the body of the leader, who was plastered against me. No matter where I moved my foot (remember the sardines), I was being sweated upon. It was just a bit distracting. I tried to take a deep breath and unplaster my nostrils, to no avail. I tried to get some air through my mouth. I don't think I've ever tried to inhale steam through my mouth before. The sweaty, smelly steam tasted like I imagine a dirty sock would. My lungs didn't seem to enjoy this experience, either.

I forced myself to get back to paying attention. It was a timely idea. We were about eight people into the group; about 25 minutes had passed. My new favorite words had become "all my relations." I was listening to these young and old men alike speak about the women in their lives, especially their mothers. It was difficult not to feel the love, high energy, and peace in the hut. I was moved to tears. So, now I'm sweating like a pig and crying…does the word dehydration come to mind?

At last, it was my son's turn. He took his time gathering his thoughts and began with his gratitude for being welcomed to the Sweat and for everyone's good wishes. He then proceeded to talk about his love for me and my unconditional love for him. I never expected to hear words like his from either of my sons, only because my boys just aren't usually that openly emotional and sensitive, in my experience. But the energy and the tone in the hut set the stage, and he embraced the moment. He expressed gratitude for my love when he didn't love anyone, including himself, during his drug addiction. When he was the worst to me, I still loved him with all my heart. I'm glad he recognized this, and I appreciate that he would share this with strangers. He prayed for his father and brother and all of his family. His sentiments were expressed eloquently and from the heart. I was so proud and grateful! After about ten more minutes, they finally came to me. I had all of these thoughts I wanted to express and so much emotion! Unfortunately, there was this voice in my head saying, "Make it short and sweet, sister, then you can get out of here!" I don't know why, but I listened to this voice and made a short, compact, heartfelt offering. I offered my prayer for my brothers and sister who were no longer on this earth. Then I offered prayer for my twin sister, who is battling breast cancer, and my parents, who have been strong through all of these life-and-death events. I expressed gratitude for my son's recovery and hope for his continued success. It was a very short offering. I had so much more to say, but I heard that voice again. Instead of continuing, I took a deep breath and said, "All my relations."

Now that the offerings were over, I was ready to breathe again. When the leader poured more water on the rocks and they started singing again, I wasn't too happy. At this point, I closed my eyes, sat up straight, and moved my butt back so it was touching the hut wall. What a discovery I made! The wall was cool from the outside cold air! It was a miracle! I put my hands back against it. I lifted the back of my T-shirt and leaned down against it and had a quick reprieve from the heat. It was another welcome distraction. After another five minutes, the singing, drums, and flute stopped. The leader yelled,

"Door," and the second "flap," after about one hour, was over.

One of the guys outside sent in some jugs of water, and we all drank as much as we could. During the break, the leader explained that the last "flap" was a kind of suffering for those known and unknown who are in pain and suffering in the world. I didn't know what this meant, but by now, I had decided I was in until the end. How much more suffering could it be? I was really feeling good about myself. I felt I had faced my claustrophobia bravely, and I hoped this was the end of living my life around it. My life was being altered dramatically from this experience.

When they started bringing in the new hot rocks, I knew something was a bit different. These particular rocks looked like they were brought out from deep within the scorching sun. Not only did they have the "glow" but also that "aura" you can see around the sun on the hottest clear summer day you could imagine. They also seemed to be never ending. The leader piled them one on top of the other, so if there was any movement at all, they could fall out of the pit. When the door shut this time, I noticed the heat immediately. The sacred herbs were burned, and a little water was thrown on the rocks. The steam was almost unbearable! It began to feel as if the rocks were burning my face right off! The men were yelling their prayers; the songs were getting faster, almost frantic. I tried to move back against the hut wall for relief, but this time it was hot, too! As my face became hotter and the sweat came dripping down from everywhere, I think even my hair was sweating! I resorted, once again, to singing with the guys and trying to dance. It was very dark, so I decided to lift my T-shirt over my face to keep it from burning off, which helped, and although it created a claustrophobic feeling, my burning face was more of an issue. Actually, one of the many things I learned from this experience was not to wear contact lenses to a Sweat! They burn onto your eyeballs and become very uncomfortable.

After about ten minutes of this screaming heat (that's where the "suffering" part comes in), I just couldn't take it anymore and asked to be let out. The leader yelled, "Door," I got up and left, and right behind me came one of the young men. I guess he was too embarrassed to say he couldn't take it if somebody's mom was doing it. I presented him with the opportunity to leave, and he grabbed it.

The night had turned quite chilly, and I was dripping wet from head to toe. I listened to them yelling and praying in the hut while I drank a bottle of water and stood by the fire. Much to my chagrin, it was only about five or ten minutes later that the leader yelled, "Door," and the Sweat was over. If I had known there would be only a few more minutes, I think I would have stayed. Of course, my contacts would have been permanently melted onto my eyeballs by then, and I might have been blinded for life!

The hut quickly emptied, and everyone, except me, dove into the adjacent, unheated pool. I live in a tropical climate, swimming only in warm pools, and was sure that a heart attack would not be a good way to top the evening. My son said it felt like pins and needles, and he could actually feel each and every one of his pores closing. After everyone dried off and dressed, they each came up to me and shook my hand. They said they were glad to meet me and congratulated me on a job well done, for my first Sweat. No one expected me to make it so far, and they were not even aware of my claustrophobia! My son was truly amazed. He admitted that he had no faith that I could make any of it. He had experienced many of my claustrophobic episodes over the years.

I appreciated the Sweat experience and was honored to be a part of it. What an amazing bonding experience with my son this turned out to be! I commend the fine people who were willing to share this experience with me and for keeping this special tradition alive. I think I can understand now the idea of spiritual retreats. It was an especially purifying experience for me.

To this day, I still have this satisfied smile on my face and warmth (no pun intended) in my heart every time I think about the Sweat.

CHAPTER FIFTEEN

The weather here in Florida was finally starting to cool down, and it was time to turn the air conditioning off and open up the house. This was the time of year when everything comes alive again, including me and my boxer, Tara. We had been holed up in the cool house and cars, just going from here to there in the heat. Our morning walks and gardening needed to be done by seven o'clock because after that, the air was stifling and the sweat began to pour out from everywhere, besides the fact that breathing was even difficult (especially for dogs with short noses)!

Now, we can breathe again! We can linger in the garden in the morning, and we can walk at any time of the day and enjoy it. Life is good! I was up in my loft room that morning and decided to open up the sliding glass doors that lead out to a balcony overlooking my yard. I walked out onto the balcony to feel the cool air on my face and to see what I could see. The yard looked very green, and the pool looked very blue and cool. I could see the bass pond on the edge of the yard that was lined with small palm trees. These trees are relatively new to our yard. They are replacements for some of the trees we lost during the four hurricanes of the past years. We lost 36 trees during the first hurricane and lost count after that. The bougainvillea in the far corner of the yard was beginning to bloom. There were a couple of white birds—egrets, I think—foraging in the swale between our yard and the golf course for their breakfast. As I panned the yard, my gaze stopped on a pair of tall pine trees miraculously still standing, and this is when I saw it. I should say it saw me. I could feel it before I saw it, actually. It was a hawk. It was not unusually large, nor was it unusually small. It was staring me right in the face. Really, I felt it almost boring a hole through my eyes. It was quite strange and a bit uncomfortable. I wondered if this bird lived here in my yard and I had failed to notice it or if it was new with the cool weather. It seemed to know me, strangely. I stood there for a few minutes and even spoke to it in my usual way of speaking to the animals in my yard, and it seemed to be listening intently. After a few minutes I decided to get on with my day.

A few years ago when life had become somewhat overwhelming for me with illness, death, and addictions ingrained into the fabric of my life, I decided to save myself because I had come to understand that no one else would. I began my quest for a more peaceful, calm, centered existence where what went on in my outside world need not reflect what went on inside me. Although I was physically fit and very health conscious, I knew my blood pressure was extremely high and I had a family history of all kinds of cancers. So, I began a very slow, step-by-step process of educating myself in keeping both mental and physical stress at bay, no matter what the world was like around me. On this day of the encounter with the hawk, I had been working very hard at this process for almost three years. I was progressively getting better at focusing on positive things, living in the moment, staying centered, and all in all, enjoying my life despite the ongoing craziness of the world I lived in. In fact I was beginning to plan for the upcoming holidays when my family would all be together, which, as a mother, is always the happiest time for me. This only happens once a year, and I was excited just thinking about it. I spent my usual hour or so up in my loft room preparing for another positive day with some calm reflection and thoughts of gratitude. I was ready to continue my day with time in the garden with Tara. I took another look out the window, and the hawk was still perched on the pine tree. I guess he liked it there. Weeding, watering, planting, and fertilizing are also expressions of my new attitude toward life. It is amazing to me as I learned to focus on details and wonder about the basic things in life and nature, how I could have lived before when I never took the time to "see." Every day there are new things happening in my garden and my life, and I look forward to finding them. Tara, who likes to take her morning nap in the patch of fluffy, mondo grass I left in the garden (I planted around it), was especially interested in something up in the tree that morning. I looked up and saw that the hawk had moved from our backyard pine tree to a tree in the front yard overlooking the garden. What was this all about?

Over the next few weeks, Tara and I spent lots of time in the garden both for peace of mind (it is good therapy for me) and because I wanted it to be extra special for the coming holidays. Each morning as I opened up the house, I looked out my upstairs window and usually saw the hawk on its perch ready to start the day with us. He seemed to always be around during my quiet, reflection time, and I began to equate his presence to peace and calm and my return to focus. As the holidays came closer and I got busier, my "lessons" about being centered, focusing on the details and staying calm were taking a backseat to everything else, allowing life to intrude again and, as they have in the past, things began to get a bit overwhelming. I stopped noticing the hawk in the trees because I was too busy doing whatever. One day near Thanksgiving I was out in the front yard, bringing the trash cans up from the street with Tara, and the hawk dove down and startled us. He almost slammed right into Tara. It really startled her. To me, it was a wake-up call. This was getting a bit weird, but I got the message. I tried to take time out and return to focusing on the moment and not get carried away with the future.

It was difficult not to get excited about the next few weeks. My sons, (23 years and 25 years) who I see so rarely and only once a year together, were coming home, and I was looking forward to their hugs and learning who they were these days. I always enjoyed seeing how they interact with each other as they mature, and I just kind of soak up the warmth of it all. This year we would be taking the trip to the grandparents for Christmas to spend time with cousins, uncles, aunts, and friends.

Everyone was in a pretty good place in their lives, and expectations were high for just relaxation and enjoyment. Practicing my new life of being centered could easily go "out the window" during times like this, but I guess I was being reminded that it would be a bad plan.

Anyway, the boys came home; the house was bustling with activity; and Tara and I tried, despite it all, to continue some semblance of our morning ritual, both up in the loft room in the morning and down in the garden. Each day the hawk was in his place. We found him either in the backyard or over the garden every day. Once in a while I would look for him and not see him. But, just as I was asking Tara where she thought he might be (as if her little-pea brain actually thought anything), we would see a moving shadow across the yard or the golf course, and he would fly up and land on a tree.

A few days before Christmas, my husband got a call about his older brother being in the hospital. We were both sitting on the back porch while he took the call, and I noticed the hawk on the tall pine tree. I saw some movement out of the corner of my eye and looked at a big evergreen tree on the side of the yard, just as a very large hawk landed on one of the branches. I had never seen this one before. The hawks stared at each other for a few minutes, while my husband was still on the phone. I pointed the birds out to him just as a point of interest, but since Tara and I had not shared our "hawk" experiences, it didn't mean too much to him. All of a sudden the large hawk flew over to the smaller hawk and knocked it right off the tree. Just as it was about to hit the ground, it spread its wings and flew away. After a moment the large hawk followed. When my husband got off the phone, he announced that he was going to the hospital to visit his brother, and my older son was going with him. When they returned they said he was serious but stable, and they promised to return to visit him at the hospital right after Christmas. We packed up the cars, took the family and dogs, and headed out for our three-hour trip. All seemed well with the world.

Hugs from the boys, smiles, and the smell of holiday food—that's what this was all about. Life was how it should be. Everyone was happy. Grandparents got to know the grandkids again; cousins told each other stories; and I sat and watched it all with a feeling of peace and joy.

The phone rang at 5:15 a.m. on Christmas. My husband's brother had died. Although he had been ill for a long time, he was still relatively young, in his 50s, and death is never easy for those left behind. The ride back seemed to last forever, and the grief that enveloped the family was certainly not the anticipated holiday feeling. It was a tragedy—death usually is—and especially tragic for a Christmas morning.

Of course, since I'm still in the learning stages of my education, I was once again overwhelmed. It didn't occur to me to step back, take a deep breath, focus on the moment and not on the what ifs and if onlys. I still have a long way to go. The next morning I walked out into the back yard and didn't see the hawk. Maybe I was too busy feeling sorry for everyone and everything going on that I didn't really look well, but I didn't see him, and I felt a little panic because of it. We were all busy getting ready for the funeral services—to focus on positive things didn't seem to have a place in our program.

Anyway, the service was nice, and afterward everyone came to our home. Of course, I was busy running around trying to tend to a large group of people and certainly couldn't get it together for a time of reflection. I had to drive one of my sons to the airport in the middle of all this and then, when I returned home, I decided to breathe, focus, and reflect on the week's events. I went up to the loft room and walked out onto the balcony. I really needed to see the hawk at that time. I was depending on it to help me focus. I know this is ridiculous, since some of the focus of my recent education was the realization that one can't count on any outside influences for serenity, peace, or happiness. It all comes from within. But, at that moment, I really needed that hawk to get me back on track!

I sat on the balcony trying to focus on the good things. Although the visit with my boys wasn't exactly as planned, I was content with their hugs, their stories, and their strength, and support given to my husband, me, and the rest of the family during this sad time. They were able to show who they were in a most unique way, and I was grateful. Life is always unpredictable, and I'm grateful to have gotten at least part way in this learning experience. It helps with all of these bumps in the road. As I sat and reflected I noticed a bird fly up on the branch where my hawk usually is perched. It was too small to be my hawk, so I didn't really take much notice. I wondered what kind of bird it was and considered grabbing my binoculars, but I was too weary to get up. Suddenly it flew off the tree toward me, and I could see that it had the same markings of our hawk, practically a miniature version. It made me smile to think that maybe while I was so distracted, the big hawk from last week, the medium hawk (my teacher), and this mini hawk might be a family, and they were enjoying the holidays together.

The holidays are over; the new year has begun; and everyone is, I believe, where they are supposed to be. Tara and I have a new appreciation for the value of staying centered and being responsible for our own serenity and continue our learning experiences. Through the joy of our family being reunited and grief of losing a family member, we see that life goes on, it just "is," no matter what. Every few days now we see a hawk in the trees, sometimes the small one, sometimes our "teacher," but now it just makes me smile to see them. I don't need them to be there anymore. When I wonder where they are now, I'm overcome with a calm that gets me through the day. I am learning each day, and I am grateful.

CHAPTER SIXTEEN

She came from Alabama eating sandwiches in the backseat of my car. I was the chauffeur and she and my neighbor my passengers. We were almost home, after a nine-hour ride. It was time for her to begin her new life in sunny Florida.

This was my replacement boxer. She had big "paws" to fill. Our previous dog was a gem. I had researched extensively for a replacement and settled on a breeder in Alabama. She sent me pictures of the litter, and I chose one from the photos. My neighbor was kind enough to volunteer to accompany me on my journey. My last boxer spent lots of time at her home, and she missed her, too. She was anxious for me to get another boxer and was happy to be part of that plan.

We arrived at the kennel and wanted to see the new pup right away. The breeder let out all of the pups onto the big property, and they frolicked around us. When the breeder pointed out our choice puppy, I was heartbroken. My last boxer died because of a neurological disease that, among other things, made her limp badly. Although this puppy was full of energy, she had a marked limp.

The breeder said that she got her leg caught in the doggie door and volunteered to take us all to the vet to check her out. So, my neighbor, the breeder, all of the pups, and I climbed into a truck and drove over to the local vet. She checked them all out and gave them all the okay. She assured me that the new pup would be good as new soon. I didn't know what to do. I really wasn't comfortable knowing that the pup was starting out with a limp. I was very sensitive to that affliction at the moment. So, I asked if any of the other pups were available. All were spoken for except one. This one had similar features of the original choice, but a few very noticeable differences in demeanor. I had noticed this one during the frolicking. She was consistently running the opposite way of the rest of the pack. She would just come back for enough time to jump on one of them or give them a quick nip. She was quite a wild one. The breeder said she had actually bitten the tip of an ear off her brother, who would grow up to be a champion. Luckily, they crop the ears of some of these champion boxers. So, my choice was a calm, limping pup or a maniac. We decided to sleep on it and make the decision in the morning. It was a difficult decision. We were about to enter our driveway. It was time to wake up my sleeping neighbor and the little maniac in the backseat. Let the games begin!

So, my son was coming home the next day from his 30 days in the drug rehab facility. This was the dog he was going to raise and take to college with him. Until then they would both be living with us. Since it was supposed to be his dog, he wanted to name her. When he arrived home he told us he had chosen the name carefully. Her name would be Tara. I thought that was fitting. Tara (the Terrible). But no, it was Tara, named after his therapist at rehab. He said that she was very nice and had helped him. He wanted his dog to remind him of her. So, her official name was Tara the Dog not the Therapist. Tara for short.

During the summer, my son took her to dog training. She learned well and could do the basic things quickly. Of course, she only did them if she felt like it. She often got this strange look in her eyes, and we knew to watch out. She would tear up the stairs, then turn around and run down as far as the landing and then jump to the foyer, sliding on the tile into the front den. She'd quickly get up and run into the kitchen, the family room, back into the foyer, and jump onto the couch, usually while my husband was resting on it. She would circle this way and make a few trips up and down the stairs and then she just stopped. She dropped down, completely exhausted, and slept. It was exhausting to watch. We had to protect ourselves as she got older and continued this craziness. She was getting bigger and stronger quickly.

My son had his bedroom upstairs, a loft room. The dog was not allowed on any furniture and was very good about listening (except in her moments of explosive running). Many times during the summer she chose to go up into my son's room to visit. She was house-trained very quickly, and we had no problems there. Except, for some reason, she would go up and pee in my son's bed. He would come stomping down the stairs with all of his bedclothes to put in the washing machine. This happened often, almost every day for a few weeks. We didn't know why she did this. She didn't pee anywhere else in the house, and she didn't go on any other furniture except his water bed. As time went by and we realized that my son was using drugs again, I was, in a strange way, glad to see Tara making his life a little miserable. She was the only one not tiptoeing around his addiction. I think she disapproved in her own little way, and she found a way to make it known. Tara became comic relief to me. When my son left our home for long-term rehab out west, Tara was left behind. She was my dog now. Did she miss the boy? I don't really know. She did spend a lot of time upstairs after he left. She never peed in his bed again.

We became constant companions. My son would turn 21 in this rehab. Whether he followed the plan for long-term rehab, sober living, then a responsible life of recovery on his own, or left rehab to continue his bad habits, he would not be living with us again. This was my choice, and I was adamant about it. There would not be any good reason for an able-bodied adult man to be living at home with his parents. So, Tara and I systematically went through every corner of his room, closet, and bathroom and cleaned it out. We threw out all of the drug paraphernalia, hundreds of CDs with negative "kill your mama" kind of messages, and most things I couldn't identify as necessities of life. Tara sniffed out some stuff I never would have found. She was pretty helpful. There were boxes of trash and shocking discoveries that I don't think I need to describe.

So, now what will we do with this room? The last big part of the cleanup was yet to come. During the horrible days of my son's addiction in our home, I had lots of bad experiences in this room. I often caught him lying on his bed using, and it was heartbreaking to watch. Afterward was even worse. I once found him sobbing in his bed, and he begged me for help. That was the bed I often thought I would find him dead in, in the mornings when he didn't answer my wake-up calls. Anyway, the bed had to go, and I knew just how I would do it. The bed was sawed into many pieces and put into the trash. It was kind of a statement for me. There is no going back to this in this room, in this house.

Shortly thereafter, I had the burgundy and hunter green walls painted with beautiful blues and a natural beige. I added some nice, cheery furniture and brought some roses up from my garden. I added some shelves, where I have pleasant pictures of my family taken when we were a happy family, and nice, soothing pictures put up on the walls. I opened up the sliding glass doors out to the balcony to get the awful smells out and fresh air in. I was determined to clear out all of the bad energy.

Tara, the crazy dog, began to change. Yes, she was very slowly maturing, but still very wild. When I began to do my morning journaling and meditations upstairs, a strange thing happened. As soon as I sat down, Tara would come upstairs, no matter what she was into or chewing on at the time; she settled at my feet and didn't get up until I was ready to go back downstairs. She never interrupted my morning ritual. That is how I learned that I could use her breathing for one of my focus exercises. It was like she was meditating, too.

Although her crazy side was unpredictable, Tara's comic relief was well received by all of us. My husband, who was never much of a dog lover, seemed to enjoy her antics. Over the past few years there had been a lot of sadness and instability in our family due to unexpected death, illnesses, and disability. When my husband encountered an unexpected injury requiring two surgeries, months of rehabilitation, and the possibility of having to give up a career of over 30 years, there was the potential for another downward spiral. Although our world did change, it could have been worse. It was at this time that Tara began her unexpected alignment with my husband. We spent the days together, but when my husband was home, she began to very slowly move her attention to him. At first, she would just go over to him and rest her chin on his lap. Then she would slowly put one of her paws up onto the couch next to him. He would rub her head, and eventually both paws were up. I, of course, had to put my foot down on this behavior because of the no-furniture rule. Tara began to curl up by his feet instead of mine. He began to notice her more when he came home, and they began a sit, stay, treat routine. It seemed that she could tell he was sad and out of sorts, and it was like she was there for him. He liked this and they became close. She always seemed to know what to do.

We all liked Tara. We liked her when she was calm and supportive. We even liked her when she was wild and crazy. She had just turned four years old and seemed to be growing out of some of her puppy stuff. Finally, we could almost trust her moves. It was at this time that she seemed to be out of sorts, so I took her in for a checkup. The result: she had cancer. It was time to step back and take a deep breath again. I could go into my previous unfocused, negative depression, or I could use what I had learned these past few years. Again, I took a deep breath and evaluated the situation. We decided to try one round of chemo. The vet assured us that dogs on chemo are different than people. They do not lose their hair, and if they do not have a bad reaction the first week, they can go into remission and have the same quality of life that they are used to.

I decided to focus on having a good time with her each day and not worry about the future. We went to visit Grandma and Grandpa. We went to visit all of her dog cousins around the state, and we spent lots of time out in the garden, mine and my neighbor's. She chased squirrels with a bit less vigor and was still attentive to all the local lizards. I made it a point to sit with her a lot, and we talked a lot about life. (She listened, I talked.) Dogs live in the moment, not planning the future or reliving the past, and I learned a lot from her in those days. She didn't know and didn't care that her life on earth was limited. She enjoyed every minute of every day. I tried my best to go with her flow. When her cancer came back four months later and we had to put her to sleep, it was sad. But I had spent the time with her doing fun, positive things without letting the fear of the future invade our good energy, and we really made the most of our time together. What a fine lesson to learn!

It has only been a few weeks since Tara has been gone. You often hear people say that things happen for a reason, or we wonder what our purpose is here on earth. When I think about Tara, although I am sad, she still makes me smile. Tara was here with us for our darkest times, with that crazy look in her eyes, her wild moments, her comic relief when we really needed it, and her constant understanding companionship. I am a different person with my new perspective and plan. There will always be some crisis or chaos. But things are okay now. Tara was here when we needed her. Maybe she was Tara the therapist after all!

CHAPTER SEVENTEEN

Fast forward four years...

His 6'1" frame was imposing. The black Calvin Klein suit, black dress shirt, and blue-and-silver-striped tie he wore agreed with his confident yet soft demeanor. At the age of 24, I'm sure to the young women he was "hot." I'm his mom, so I'll reserve my opinion. He's just my sweet boy. We were up on the stage in a big hall, waiting for the meeting to begin. My son motioned to me to come to the podium with him. It was time. He introduced himself to the more than two hundred people in the room with the usual fellowship greeting and all replied their greeting. He stood for a moment to collect his thoughts and then began.

"My mom flew across the country to help me celebrate this third anniversary of my being clean and sober. This is my mom. I love my mom."

These anniversaries are a special time we spend together. I am there, no matter what. This year, I had broken a rib a few days before the 6 hour flight but that would not stop me. We don't forget, but we are grateful. I am always impressed with how calm, uninhibited, and mature my son seems, speaking in front of large numbers of his peers. The first year I was overwhelmed. My speech was exactly three words: I am grateful! This year I graduated to about 30 seconds of proud and grateful. He spoke for another minute. In conclusion, he said, "If any of you would like to hug my mom after the meeting, please be gentle. She broke a rib three days ago."

So, miracles do happen. There is always hope. His new, clean-and-sober life and peace and serenity are his miracles, his "stuff." I am proud of his new choices and am well-aware that they are his choices and choices can change. He is responsible for his choices, and I am responsible for mine.

Now at home each morning I awake and am grateful for whatever the day has to offer. I go out to my garden and am excited to see what is blooming that day. I have planted, fertilized, watered, and loved, and now I am just watching what happens. I am letting things grow.

My own sheepish smile can be detected on my face, and a joy comes from my heart when I see how nurturing and allowing can work. The feelings are similar when I think about my son and his "miracles," my garden and its wonders, and my own transformation to nurturing and allowing.

As has been the case for most of my life, there is extreme chaos and craziness in my day-to-day life once again. I'm good with that. I have hope, and I have my new spirit.

I think I'll go out and float in the pool and watch the clouds go by for a while. Chaos will be there for later.

Epilogue

My thoughts, emotions, highs and lows, hard work, and transformation are just that. Mine. Addiction is a disease not only of the addict but of the family. I cannot presume to know what goes on in the minds of others. *Sweat* is what came from within the confines of my mind and my experience. My family was equally touched by this experience, and each has his/her own story. I cannot tell their stories. Maybe someday they will.

I wish all of you stories with happy endings.

LaVergne, TN USA
06 April 2010
178411LV00001B/1/P